the greatest story

JESUS

Lutheran Study Bible edition

the greatest story

JESUS

Allen R. Hilton

Foreword by Mark Allan Powell

AUGSBURG FORTRESS

THE GREATEST STORY
JESUS
Lutheran Study Bible edition

Copyright © 2011 Augsburg Fortress. All rights reserved. Except for brief quotations in critical articles or reviews, no part of this book may be reproduced in any manner without prior written permission from the publisher. For more information, visit: www.augsburgfortress.org/copyrights or write to: Permissions, Augsburg Fortress, Box 1209, Minneapolis, MN 55440-1209.

Scripture quotations, unless otherwise marked, are from New Revised Standard Version Bible, copyright ©1989 Division of Christian Education of the National Council of Churches of Christ in the United States of America. Used by permission. All rights reserved.

ISBN: 978-1-4514-0153-0

Writer: Allen R. Hilton
Foreword: Mark Allan Powell
Illustrators: David L. Hanson, Julie Lonneman
Cover design: Alisha Lofgren
Interior design: Ivy Palmer Skrade
Typesetting: PerfecType, Nashville, TN

The paper used in this publication meets the minimum requirements of American National Standard for Information Sciences—Permanence of Paper for Printed Library Materials, ANSI Z329.48-1984.

Manufactured in the U.S.A.

14 13 12   2 3 4 5 6 7 8 9 10

CONTENTS

About our writers

Allen R. Hilton is a scholar pastor. He currently serves as Teaching Minister at Wayzata Community Church, a 2,700-member United Church of Christ (UCC) congregation in Wayzata, Minnesota. Previously he was Senior Minister at Plymouth Church, UCC in Seattle, Washington, and Minister of Christian Formation at the Congregational Church of New Canaan, Connecticut. Before entering the professional ministry, Hilton taught New Testament on the faculty of Yale Divinity School. His missional purpose is to bring Christians who balk at the Bible into the large and involving world that book holds, and to the Christ who lies at its center. He lives in Minnetonka, Minnesota with his wife, Liz, and their two sons, Sam and Isaac.

Mark Allan Powell is Professor of New Testament at Trinity Lutheran Seminary and an internationally known biblical scholar. He is editor of the HarperCollins Bible Dictionary and author of more than 25 books on the Bible, including *Fortress Introduction to the Gospels*. He has also written in the areas of spiritual formation (*Loving Jesus*), stewardship (*Giving To God*), and preaching (*What Do They Hear?: Bridging the Gap between Pulpit and Pew*). Powell's DVD series *How Lutherans Understand the Bible* has received widespread use throughout the ELCA and was excerpted for inclusion in *Lutheran Study Bible* (Augsburg Fortress, 2009).

FOREWORD

Mark Allan Powell

What makes for a truly great story? People find stories appealing for many different reasons, but the truly great stories tend to do certain things.

First, they engage us: they might make us laugh; they might make us cry; they might frighten us; they might inspire us; but, in one way or another, they make us care!

Second, they surprise us: characters make unexpected decisions; events take an unanticipated turn—things never go quite the way we thought they would.

And, third—sometimes—a truly great story will transform us: it may reveal something to us, something about ourselves or about life or love or the world in general; it may change the way we think or feel—even the way we act.

A great story is one that grips us and does something to us. After hearing such a story, we know can never be the same again.

The story of Jesus is a great story. It has been called "the greatest story ever told," and I think it lives up to that claim. You may think you already know this story. You may think you know it well, and perhaps you do. But I have been reading the story of Jesus, repeatedly, for many years now and, still, it never fails to engage, surprise, and transform me.

A Rewarding Story Experience

Here are a few tips that might make your encounter with the story of Jesus more rewarding:

1. Let the story unfold. Don't get distracted by peripheral questions or concerns. You may wonder: Did all of this actually happen? Is there any proof, historically? You may ask: Am I supposed to agree with everything Jesus says? Is this really what the church believes? These are legitimate issues that you may want to explore sometime, but right now I would encourage you to just let the story unfold. Whatever you think about history or doctrine or religion or politics or any number of other things that might come to mind as you encounter this story, let the story be what it is. Find out where it wants to take you and discover what it does to you.

2. Imagine the story is new to you. Try to hear the story as though you are hearing it for the first time. Of course, you know parts of it already. I'm sure you already know (spoiler alert) that Jesus gets crucified and I'm pretty sure you also know what happens after that. Nevertheless, stories are usually best received when we experience them the way they were intended to be experienced, and most of us know how to use our imagination to re-create such an experience. My wife cries every time we watch the movie *E.T.:*

The Extra-Terrestrial (Universal Pictures, 1982), when it gets to the part where you are supposed to think that E.T. is dead. I almost want to tell her, "We've seen this before. He's not really dead." But of course she knows that; she's just pretending she doesn't know so that the movie will affect her the way it was intended to affect people. We all have powerful imaginations. I recommend you put yours to work when encountering the story of Jesus.

3. Participate in the story. Sometimes the best way to experience a story is from within, as one of the characters participating in the action. We do this through empathy, identifying with various characters in the tale and experiencing everything from their perspective. Again, this takes imagination: when you read the story of Jesus, imagine that you are one of the shepherds told of his birth, one of the fishermen called to follow him, one of the Pharisees he labels a hypocrite, one of the women who discovers his empty tomb. How do you feel about what happens? What do you think of this man Jesus—and what does he think of you?

Four Testimonies, One Story

Remember, too, that there are four stories of Jesus. They have been woven together in our minds, and we don't usually pay much attention to which story does what (for example: the shepherds are in Luke's Christmas story, but the wise men are in Matthew's).

In this book, Allen Hilton does a magnificent job of introducing us to these four stories of Jesus with a clear focus on the one, truly great story that unfolds when they are read together. Every now and then he alerts us to something that is particularly true of one book in the Bible but not the others; sometimes he even indicates how the Gospels relate different versions of an event, in ways that make decidedly different points. These observations add depth, as do the Background Files and other special features you will find scattered throughout the book. They reveal that the story has layers. There is much to be found on the surface but, every now and then, we will become aware that there is much more to be discovered in these four different testimonies to the greatest story ever told.

Over and Over Again

I will conclude by telling you something about myself that I am not usually inclined to disclose. It pertains to my personal devotional life, which is personal and not something I regard as anyone else's business. But let this be my testimony . . .

Our church follows a three-year lectionary. Every year that we are in Series A, I take one day each month and read the Gospel of Matthew straight through from beginning to end. When it is Series C, I do the same thing with the Gospel of Luke. And, during the Series B year, I read both Mark and John (which, combined, are about the length of either Matthew or Luke). I read the books out loud and it always takes about four hours to read either Matthew or Luke or both Mark and John.

I've been doing this for 35 years. You might think that, by now, I would have reached a saturation point. It hasn't happened. The story doesn't change from month to month or year to year, but I do—and the story still engages me, surprises me, and transforms me as though I were reading it for the first time.

There are lots of great stories and I love them all, from Shakespeare to Dr. Seuss—comic books, fairy tales, Greek myths, mystery novels, Winnie-the-Pooh, and everything in-between. I love them all, but I have never found any other story that I would want to read out loud, every month for 35 years.

It is not just that this story changed me once, when I first heard it. That is true, but there is something more: this story changes me every time I hear it and I know, every time I open the Bible to read it again, I am not going to be the same when I am done. It happens over and over again, and that is enough for me to call this story of Jesus the greatest story ever told.

WHO IS THIS JESUS?

1

Four Gospels

These are written so that you may come to believe . . .

So that you will believe

- What do you most want to learn from this study?

FOUR GOSPELS, ONE JESUS

Encountering Jesus of Nazareth radically changed the people who were fortunate enough to know him. He healed them, taught them, inspired faith, and showed them a whole new way to live.

The rest of us encounter Jesus, not on the ground in Galilee, but through the inspired stories others told about him. Four decades after Jesus' ministry, a Christian author gathered many of these little stories into the large story of Jesus' ministry that we call the "Gospel of Mark." Over the next three decades other authors did the same thing, and from them we got the Gospels of Matthew, Luke, and John.

Each author paints his unique portrait of Jesus to help his own community live faithfully, but John's words apply to all four: "These are written so that you may come to believe that Jesus is the Messiah, the Son of God, and that through believing you may have life in his name" (20:31).

GOD'S SON (Mark 1:1-2)

Mark has barely picked up his pen when he blurts out his project: "The beginning of the good news of Jesus Christ, the Son of God." And from that opening sentence, Mark sprints breathlessly, like an excited child, through his story of Jesus (the Greek word for "immediately" appears forty-one times in sixteen chapters). In rapid succession we see Jesus calling disciples, healing sick and troubled people, teaching, reaching out to forgotten people, confronting religious gatekeepers, dying, rising.

- Are you more like those who are confused about why Jesus came, or more like those who seem to have it figured out? Why?
- As you read and discuss, you'll both learn facts and be challenged in faith. How will you manage the side-by-side activities of your head and your heart?

Mark's claim in 1:1 that Jesus is God's son plays out ironically and mysteriously. We readers know it right away. At the baptismal waters, God confirms it to Jesus: "You are my Son, the Beloved; with you I am well pleased" (1:9-11). The evil spirits even know Jesus' true identity (3:11). But the people around Jesus keep guessing wrongly. Some Jewish leaders think he's from the devil (3:22), and the people think he's some kind of prophet (8:27-28). Even his disciples are confused. Peter guesses that Jesus is the Messiah, but then shows that he doesn't understand (8:29-33). Jesus seems to relish the mystery: he several times even shushes his would-be publicists.

In the end, the words of 1:1 are given back to us from the unlikeliest of lips. His disciples and the expectant masses have watched Jesus heal hordes, calm the sea, and feed thousands with a little bread, but it's not until he breathes his last breath from the dark cross that someone most unexpected finally recognizes him: A Roman guard sees him die and says, "Truly this man was God's Son!" (15:39).

How can a son of God die? In this poignant moment at the cross, we learn that Jesus lives out a different sort of divinity than anyone anticipated. We might have expected political power and earthly rule. As we follow Jesus' story, we will learn just how different this son of God is.

LONG-AWAITED KING (Matthew 1:1-17)

When you want to grab people's attention, do you read to them from an inventory list or phone book? Not likely. But Matthew begins his Gospel with a seventeen-verse, forty-two-generation family tree. It's like reading the Jerusalem phone book. Scintillating! So why would he begin this way?

Matthew's Jesus lives in a Jewish world. These opening verses trace Jesus' family line to Abraham (see Genesis) through the great King David. In his Sermon on the Mount, Jesus will tell his followers, "Do not think that I have come to abolish the law or the prophets; I have come not to abolish but to fulfill" (5:17). Throughout the Gospel, Matthew will take pains to demonstrate from Hebrew Scripture (our Old Testament) that Jesus is the expected Messiah. Matthew litters his book with the phrase "as it is written," followed by a quotation from Hebrew Scripture. When Jesus sends his disciples out to minister he will tell them "go rather to the lost sheep of the house of Israel" (10:6). In this Jewish world a genealogy has authority.

There are surprises, though. This Gospel speaks straight to Jewish Christian sensibilities, but even Jesus' family tree hints at a widening of God's reach to the whole world, with four Gentile women in the mix. In chapter 2, wise men will travel from foreign nations to see the newborn king (2:1-12). The first of Jesus' friends to the empty tomb of his resurrection will be women. Then, at Gospel's end, the risen Jesus will send his followers out to "make disciples of all nations" (28:19).

The strangest thing about Matthew's genealogy is that it stops just before the finish line. It seems simple. Jesus is a son of a son of David and therefore a proper candidate to be Israel's expected Messiah. But there's a catch. After forty-one times naming so-and-so the father of so-and-so, just at the crucial time Matthew changes form. He writes ". . . and Eleazar the father of Matthan, and Matthan the father of Jacob, and Jacob the father of Joseph the husband of Mary, of whom Jesus was born, who is called the Messiah" (1:15-16).

Joseph is the husband of Jesus' mama. But who will be the daddy? Stay tuned!

The message of Matthew

- What do you think of the fact that Jesus was born into a Jewish family and learned the Scriptures of the Jewish people?

JESUS ON THE BIG STAGE
(Luke 1:1-4)

Luke's Gospel starts as ancient histories (and modern scholarly books) begin: by making space for it amid the many books that already exist. From him we learn that many others have written down lives of Jesus—more than even the four Gospels in the New Testament. But rather than simply handing one of those to Theophilus, he elects "to write an orderly account for you, most excellent Theophilus, so that you may know the truth concerning the things about which you have been instructed."

Luke may be the most educated author in the New Testament. His Greek is, with the author of Hebrews, the best in the New Testament. This brief introduction signals that Luke knew a wider literary world than just the Hebrew Bible and religious books. Some have noticed that Luke's opening resembles the introductions to Roman history books. In the course of his Gospel and its sequel, the Acts of the Apostles, he refers easily to poets and philosophers, even crafting his portrait of Jesus and the apostles to resemble those philosophers.

The message of Luke

• What do you think of the idea that Jesus lives in and through the church?

Luke has an advantage in our New Testament: he gets to write a sequel. The Gospel of Luke is twenty-four chapters long, and it tells about Jesus' birth, life, death, and resurrection. But Acts begins strangely, by Luke summarizing his Gospel's contents as "all that Jesus did and taught from the beginning" (Acts 1:1). But this phrase in Greek has the sense of what Jesus *began to do and teach*. So, in Acts 1:1-11, Luke makes an important point: Jesus' story didn't end with his resurrection. He keeps living in the church. That's why, when Peter and John stand courageously before persecutors (Acts 4:1-13) and Stephen prays for his tormentors' forgiveness (Acts 7:60), they look like Jesus. His life is living out through them. The Apostle Paul captures this truth: "I have been crucified with Christ; and it is no longer I who live, but it is Christ who lives in me" (Galatians 2:19-20).

The message of John

• John's Gospel claims—and the Christian church agrees—that Jesus is God "in the flesh." How can this be?

GOD IN THE FLESH (John 1:1-18)

Who is Jesus? The first three Gospels answer this question using a blend of Jesus' actions with guesses by the people around him. John goes at the question much more directly. Seven times Jesus simply tells us, "I am . . ."—"the bread of life . . . the light of the world . . . the gate . . . the good shepherd . . . the resurrection and the life . . . the way, and the truth, and the life," and ". . . the true vine."

But the strongest claim about Jesus in all of Scripture comes in the first verses of John. Here, Jesus is no less than the Word, who was "with God" and "was God." Through this Word God created the cosmos. In this man of Nazareth, the bright, glorious, eternal Word "became flesh and lived among us, and we have seen his glory (1:14)." Jesus lives out the bright light of God. John will say it again in another way: "No one has ever seen God. It is God the only Son, who is close to the Father's heart, who has made him known" (1:18).

What a way to start a book! The verb that is translated "lived among us" (1:14) could be translated "pitched a tent in our midst." Imagine a huge field of a thousand tents at a Scout jamboree. Now imagine that it's your job to find the one that has a lamp inside. Tents spread out as far as the eye can see, but which one holds the lamp? In your search, a pinhole or two would help—openings in the tent that let light out. In John's Gospel, those pin-holes are called "signs," and they help people to see Jesus' glory—to discover where the light of God is. After Jesus turns water to wine at a wedding, John tells us, "Jesus did this, the first of his signs, in Cana of Galilee, and revealed his glory; and his disciples believed in him" (2:11).

After peppering his Gospel with seven of these signs, John will tell us that this has merely been a small sample. Jesus did many more signs! "But these are written so that you may come to believe that Jesus is the Messiah, the Son of God, and that through believing you may have life in his name" (20:31).

- Each Gospel asks, "Who is Jesus?" As we begin our journey through his life, how do you answer that question?

Background Files

Titles and Authors. Gospel writers didn't sign their stories, so why do we call them Matthew, Mark, Luke, and John?

Early in the second century, a Christian named Papias wrote, "**Mark**, having become the interpreter of Peter, wrote down accurately whatsoever he remembered. It was not, however, in exact order that he related the sayings or deeds of Christ. For he neither heard the Lord nor accompanied Him . . ." (Eusebius, *Church History* 3.39).

Papias continued, "**Matthew** put together the oracles [of the Lord] in the Hebrew language, and each one interpreted them as best he could."

The Apostle Paul names a companion called **Luke** (Colossians 4:14; 2 Timothy 4:11; Philemon verse 24), and part of Paul's travel in Acts is narrated in the first person plural ("we"). By the late second century, many Christian authors name Luke the author of this Gospel and Acts.

Early in the second century, a Christian named Polycarp named the Apostle **John** the author of the Fourth Gospel.

Article. Read "The Gospels and Acts" on pages 1599–1600 in *Lutheran Study Bible*.

PICTURING THE STORY

As you watch the story unfold in the video, consider:

- Which three Gospels are most alike? Why?
- What questions are raised for you about the story of Jesus?
- What are you looking forward to learning more about?
- Does it surprise or disturb you that the story of Jesus is told in four different versions (Gospels)? Why or why not?
- The word *gospel* comes from a Greek word meaning "good news." From what you know about Jesus, what makes his story "good news"?

SINGING THE STORY

Just as the Psalms were the songbook of the people of Israel, so Christians have written and sung hymns and songs to convey the story of Jesus and its meaning.

"Come Thou Long-Expected Jesus" (Charles Wesley, 1707–1778)

Come, thou long-expected Jesus,
born to set thy people free;
from our fears and sins release us;
let us find our rest in thee.
Israel's strength and consolation,
hope of all the earth thou art
dear desire of every nation,
joy of every longing heart.

What do you expect of Jesus?

MARK IT

Choose one or more of the following passages to read during the coming week. Mark your readings using the marking method shown below.

Mark 1:1-3   Hebrews 1:1-9
John 1:1-14   Romans 1:16-17

Marking Your Bible

Make notes about the questions and insights you have as you read your Bible. The following symbols might be helpful.

*   A chapter or verse important to me
!   A new idea
√   A passage to memorize
?   Something not clear to me
∞   God's love
℗   A promise from God
≈   Something that connects with my experience
†   My relationship with God
↔   My relationships with others

Next Time
Use the following suggestions to prepare for Session 2 and to review Session 1.

Read the Introductions to each of the four Gospels in *Lutheran Study Bible*:
• Matthew, pages 1604–1606
• Mark, pages 1659–1660
• Luke, pages 1694–1695
• John, pages 1752–1753

Read the following passages from the Gospels:
• Matthew, chapters 1 and 2
• Mark 1:1-8
• Luke, chapters 1 and 2
• John 1:1-18

Gospels Reading Plan
If you wish to read one entire Gospel or all four Gospels during the sixteen weeks of this study, follow this weekly reading plan.

Week 1: Matthew 1:1—2:23; Mark 1:1-8; Luke 1:1—2:52; John 1:1-51

2

GOD IS WITH US
Birth Narratives

To you is born this day in the city of David a Savior, who is the Messiah, the Lord.

Birth stories matter. I've heard parents tell their child, "We knew you would be a thinker when you put your hand under your chin during the ultrasound!" We invest great importance in what happens first. That's why ancient authors characterized their heroes by narrating special birth stories.

The Bible's story of Jesus' birth arrives in two packages: Luke tells it through Mary, who hears an angel and says a profound "Yes!" to the purposes of God: "Here am I, the servant of the Lord; let it be with me according to your word" (Luke 1:38). Matthew tells it through Joseph, who also heeds the word of an angel and does what is right. From such faithful parents comes the baby Jesus, who will be no less than "Emmanuel, . . . God is with us" (Matthew 1:23). Soon, wise men from the East will come along with gifts.

O come let *us* adore him!

A RIGHTEOUS DADDY (Matthew 1:18-25)
Dreamers named Joseph finally fare very well in the Bible, but they don't travel an easy road. The one with a technicolor jacket eventually rose in Pharaoh's court by interpreting dreams for him (Genesis 37–50), but only after enduring slavery and prison time. The carpenter of Matthew's story wore much more drab attire, we would imagine, but he got his dream too—and just at the right excruciating time.

Joseph has just heard Mary say words that send a chill through any chaste fiancé: "I'm pregnant." How could this be? And what should he do? The law of Moses licenses Joseph to have Mary stoned in the town square for her betrayal. But he is a "righteous man" and "unwilling to expose her to public disgrace" (1:19), so he plans to end the engagement quietly. Oh, the agony of infidelity!

Imagine the night before Joseph would tell Mary of his decision. Each of us has known this sort of tortured, sleepless night. When Joseph finally dozes off, he dreams of an angel visitor. "Joseph, . . . do not be afraid to take Mary as your wife, for the child conceived in her is from the Holy Spirit" (1:20). Do not be afraid, says the angel, and fear must be in his tortured mix of emotions—fear of a far different future than he expected. And the angel won't give back his normal future: "She will bear a son, and you are to name him Jesus, for he will save his people from their sins." This sort of reassurance may not lead to sound sleep, but it is far better than what he thought before.

Joseph: "You want me to do what?"

- Has God ever led your life in an unexpected direction? How did you recognize that the prompt came from God?

Joseph marries Mary ("he took her as his wife") and gets on the roller coaster. He'll have another angel dream that sends the family to safe haven in Egypt (2:13). Then when the grown-up Jesus preaches in his hometown, Nazarene neighbors will deride Jesus, "He's just Joseph's boy, right?"

To you and me, Joseph will ever and always be a shining example of a kind of faith that does not get off when the ride gets bumpy.

A HEAVEN-FAVORED MAMA
(Luke 1:26-38, 46-55)
Luke plays Mary's side of the split-screen video. A poor, newly engaged, teenage girl lives her own nondescript life in Nazareth, counting down the days 'til her very normal wedding and married life.

Then an angel interrupts. "Greetings, favored one! The Lord is with you" (Luke 1:28). Throughout Scripture, angels evoke fear, but Mary is at least as puzzled as she is scared. What?! How could God choose me?

And if the greeting confused her, what came next was baffling: "You're going to have a baby boy, and he is going to reign over God's people as the great King David did. By the way: call him Jesus, will you?" To her great credit, the virgin girl blurts out the obvious question: "How?!" The angel answers to Mary's satisfaction.

Mary's ultimate answer to the angel puts her in honored company. She sounds like Israel's greatest leaders—like Moses answering God at the burning bush (Exodus 3:4) and Isaiah in the temple (Isaiah 6:8). How could she have known that during all those Scripture stories with her family, God was training her for her own big story? But this girl's words echo theirs: "Here am I, the servant of the Lord" (Luke 1:38).

Mary: "Let it be . . ."

- To what sort of "Mary moment" may God be calling you?

As for her next words, the God-blessed son will repeat them in a far-off garden with sweat rolling and tears streaming. Maybe Mary told stories of her chat with the angel. Or maybe the apple doesn't fall far from the tree. Whatever the cause, her "Let it be with me according to your word" sounds a lot like his "Thy will be done!" Like mother, like Son.

- We all wonder what kind of people God uses. What do you learn about faithful living from Joseph and Mary?

It's no wonder Mary is surprised. God has done an unexpected thing. But strange as it is, she says yes, and she ponders the wonder-full mystery of God. As her soul "magnifies the Lord," she echoes the words of Hannah, another saint of Israel (1 Samuel 2:1-10).

I wonder: for what bigger-than-we-imagined story is God training you and me?

THE CENTER MOVES (Luke 2:1-20)

Joseph and Mary live out at the edge of the Roman world. But the most famous part of the greatest story ever told begins at its center. The Roman Emperor Augustus rides aloft in litters carried by slaves. Well-to-do clients endure long lines in hopes of a few seconds in his presence. The most powerful people in the world know not to cross him. All the world bows down to their "Savior" and "Lord," the Emperor Augustus. When Caesar says, "Jump!" they all ask, "How high?"

One day the man at the center of the world wants to know how many minions he has in Syria. So Caesar's people at the center call Governor Quirinius's people at the outer edge, and suddenly a nowhere and nobody couple named Mary and Joseph get their turn to ask "How high?" She is "with child" and should not travel, but Joseph and Mary are the people, and Caesar-at-the-center is the emperor, so they set out. Their route tracks through the hill country of Galilee, then east across the Jordan and back west again at the Dead Sea. It's not easy travel. But they make their long, winding way to Bethlehem, hometown of Joseph's great, great, great grand-daddy David, who once was king.

That's when something strange happens: way off at the edge of the world, heavenly angels terrify peasant shepherds, but then comfort them with startling words: "I am bringing you good news of great joy for all the people: to you is born this day in the city of David a Savior, who is the Messiah, the Lord" (Luke 2:10-11).

Life having been slow out at the edge of the world, the shepherds immediately drop everything and sprint to town, where they find the poor family in the stable that was all they could find.

They arrive to find Joseph and Mary and a baby "wrapped in bands of cloth and lying in a manger." The Savior is in Bethlehem. And as peasant shepherds adore a peasant carpenter's son in a rude stable with no one else watching, there is cause to believe that the center of the universe has moved.

WISE MEN (Matthew 2:1-12)

Another sign that the center has moved comes next in Matthew's story, when "wise men from the East" make their way—not to the great city of Rome, but to the little town of Bethlehem. Angels have been our guides so far. One told Joseph (in a dream) that his son would save his people from their sins. Another told Mary that their son would rule the people Israel. Yet another sent shepherds to the manger.

Now the heavens speak differently as a peculiar star sends eastern astronomers on a journey. From distant lands, wise men venture to visit the baby. When they inquire in Jerusalem, "Where is the child who has been born king of the Jews?" (2:2) any Jew would have been reminded of "the Messiah."

And yet Jerusalem is hardly ready for the question. For nearly six centuries, since the exile to Babylon, Israel has wondered when God would renew David's dynasty. So when King Herod asks chief priests and scribes where the Messiah would be born, they come up with the answer easily. But these

The Savior is born in Bethlehem

- How would you say that Jesus' birth has re-centered the universe? How has Jesus' birth "rocked your world"?

- The Greek word translated *angel* also means "messenger." Who or what are God's angels in your life?

Wise Men: "Where is the child who has been born king of the Jews?"

• What do you think it means that those outside Jesus' own people recognize he was born to be king?

leaders are conspicuously uninterested. They do not hitch their camels and get in line behind the magi. Nor do the people. The only real interest comes from Herod himself, who fakes a desire to pay the boy-king homage, but really (and tragically) hopes to extinguish the potential competition.

Herod has misjudged the nature of the new king's reign. But a hint arrives in the gifts these wise foreigners bring. Gold befits a king, of course. But frankincense and myrrh, while expensive, are spices that speak of death. T. S. Eliot poses this mystery in his poem "The Gift of the Magi." There the wise ones, after their arduous journey, ask themselves "were we led all that way for / Birth or Death?"

Only time will tell.

Background Files

Messiah. Israel's expectation of a Messiah ("anointed one") joins God's promise to David of an everlasting dynasty (2 Samuel 7:1-15), with the fact that Babylonian soldiers ended that dynasty in 587 B.C.E. (2 Kings 24–25).

Birth Story Distinctions. While most nativity pageants bring shepherds and wise men into the story, Matthew and Luke each tell the story of Jesus' birth differently and with their own themes in mind.

Matthew sees Jesus' birth and life as a fulfillment of Jewish expectations. Five times he quotes Hebrew Scripture to show that these events fulfill what the prophets expected (1:23; 2:5, 15, 17-18, 23).

Luke's Jesus performs on the world stage, so here in Luke 2 and when he introduces John the Baptist in Luke 3 he names a long list of leaders over the Roman and Jewish people.

Geography. Examine the maps "The Roman Empire" and "Palestine in Jesus' Time," pages 2108–2109 in *Lutheran Study Bible*. Find Nazareth in Galilee, Bethlehem in Judea, and the city of Rome in Italy. Notice the large territory the Roman Empire controlled.

PICTURING THE STORY

As you watch the story unfold in the video, consider:

- What do you find most remarkable or intriguing in the stories surrounding the birth of Jesus?
- With which character do you most easily identify in these stories?
- What questions are raised for you?
- If you could ask any character in the birth stories a question, who would it be? What would you ask?
- What did the artist help you see in a new way?

SINGING THE STORY

Just as the Psalms were the songbook of the people of Israel, so Christians have written and sung hymns and songs to convey the story of Jesus and its meaning.

"O Little Town of Bethlehem" (Phillips Brooks, 1835–1893)
O little town of Bethlehem, how still we see thee lie!
Above thy deep and dreamless sleep the silent stars go by;
yet in thy dark streets shineth the everlasting Light.
The hopes and fears of all the years are met in thee tonight.

How silently, how silently, the wondrous Gift is giv'n!
So God imparts to human hearts the blessings of his heav'n.
No ear may hear his coming; but in this world of sin,
where meek souls will receive him, still the dear Christ enters in.

How is it that such a "silent" birth in a faraway place has had such a loud impact on the world? How do your hopes and fears meet in Jesus?

MARK IT

Choose one or more of the following passages to read during the coming week. Mark your readings using the marking method shown below.

Luke 1:46-56
Matthew 2:13-18

Luke 1:67-80
Ephesians 1:3-14

Marking Your Bible

Make notes about the questions and insights you have as you read your Bible. The following symbols might be helpful.

* ∗ A chapter or verse important to me
* ! A new idea
* √ A passage to memorize
* ? Something not clear to me
* ∞ God's love
* ℗ A promise from God
* ≈ Something that connects with my experience
* † My relationship with God
* ↔ My relationships with others

Next Time
Use the following suggestions to prepare for Session 3 and review Session 2.

Review the study notes in *Lutheran Study Bible* for:
* Matthew 1:1—4:11
* Mark 1:1-13
* Luke 1:1—4:13
* John 1:1-34

Read the following passages from the Gospels:
* Matthew 3:1—4:11
* Mark 1:4-13
* Luke 3:1—4:13
* John 1:19-34

Gospels Reading Plan
If you wish to read one entire Gospel or all four Gospels during the sixteen weeks of this study, follow this weekly reading plan.

Week 2: Matthew 3:1—4:11; Mark 1:9-45; Luke 3:1—4:13; John 2:1—3:36

THIS IS MY SON

Baptism, Calling, Temptation

3

This is my Son, the Beloved, with whom I am well pleased.

The people who encountered Jesus had to decipher his identity from his words and actions alone. They heard him speak, saw him act with compassion and perform wonders. But how did they estimate him? They sized him up as best they could.

In this sense alone, we Gospel readers may have an advantage. In various ways, our authors have told us who is coming (Session 1). We've heard angels use words like "Savior" and "Messiah" and wise men who inquire about the "New King" (Session 2). Now we'll hear a wild-eyed prophet shout about "One who is to come" "more powerful than I," who will "baptize with the Holy Spirit and with fire"; God himself will call Jesus his "Beloved Son"; and the Devil will begin his temptations with the words, "If you are the Son of God . . ." We get all this before Jesus says a word.

THE PROPHET (Matthew 3:1-12)

Before we meet the grown-up Jesus, we run headlong into a shouting prophet at the river's edge. John the Baptist could preach the paint off the wall—if he had a house. Instead he wears the camel's hair clothes and leather belt of a wilderness prophet. John's eyes blaze out there by the Jordan as he afflicts all the comfortable within the considerable range of his voice.

John's message is simple: "Repent, for the kingdom of heaven has come near" (3:2). Repent! Turn around! This is no convenient, cost-free forgiveness. John expects change. Religious complacency drives him crazy! He pictures the return of righteous Israel, and he'll do anything to hasten that day.

John is no mere warm-up act. The Jewish historian Josephus tells us that the sheer size of John's following scared Herod, who eventually imprisoned and executed him. Indeed, two decades after John's death and hundreds of miles northwest, the book of Acts will notice followers of John in Ephesus (18:25); and decades later John's Gospel will still need to clarify for his readers that John is not the Messiah (John 1:6-8, 15).

John the Baptist prepares the way for the unexpected God

• Can you relate to John the Baptist? Has the God you got ever been different than the God you expected?

All this makes John's announcement all the more potent: "One who is more powerful than I is coming after me; I am not worthy to carry his sandals. He will baptize you with the Holy Spirit and fire" (3:11).

Jesus will redefine power. In a strange resemblance to Herod, John may misjudge the shape of this coming One. "His winnowing fork is in his hand, and he will clear his threshing floor and will gather his wheat into the granary; but the chaff he will burn with unquenchable fire" (3:12). John expects that heads will roll and the world will be put right. He expects to ride triumphant into an age of righteousness.

Eight chapters later, from the dungeon of a petty dictator while Jesus heals diseases and teaches his followers to love their enemies, John will ask his disappointed question: "Are you the one who is to come, or are to wait for another?" (Matthew 11:2-3) Mighty John got a different Messiah than he expected!

THE BAPTISM (Matthew 3:13-17)

The clear voice of God is a rare treat in life. Mostly we muddle about, taking our lead from nudges and hints, intuitions and chance remembrances of Scripture. Moments of clarity are few.

We would hardly think we have that experience in common with Jesus. But in the Gospels, Jesus rarely hears the direct voice of God resound. Even in his times of greatest need—on the eve of his death and on the cross—the heavens are silent, and he must discern and bear up without that unambiguous certainty.

We don't know what Jesus knew of his status and mission before this moment. In Matthew's telling, John knows that something is backward, so he protests: "I need to be baptized by you" (3:14). But Jesus insists, and they both step out into the water. What does Jesus know? Has he had clear moments before?

Then clarity comes. Jesus steps from those baptismal waters and out of John's grasp, dripping wet. In that instant, he sees the heavens open, feels God's Spirit come to him, and hears God's voice ring from the heavens: "This is my Son, the Beloved, with whom I am well pleased" (Matthew 3:17).

In Jesus' baptism we can see ourselves in two very different ways: first, we might look amid the masses who trek to Jordan's waters. Like those ancient Pharisees and Sadducees, we sometimes ride along on our own false assurances: we live in a Christian nation, we belong to a church, we do our best to live a good life. But John's voice cracks our complacency and calls us to repent, turn around, find God really and live out that God-claimed life every day.

Then we see ourselves in a second way: we are not the Christ. Not close. But somehow, through grace, God calls us "beloved children." Soon in this story Jesus will teach us to pray, "Our Father. . . ." In the waters of our baptism, God has claimed us. Wonder of wonders, through the one John baptized there, the heavenly Father will be pleased with us too.

God names and claims Jesus—and us—in baptism

- Have you ever sensed that you are beloved by God? Describe that experience.

- Do you feel more comfortable being called to repent or being called "beloved child"? Why?

THE TEMPTATION (Matthew 4:1-11)

Jesus is like us in another way: his mountaintop experience gives way to life in the valley. If you've ever been on a great retreat, or experienced especially rich worship, you know this abrupt back-to-back. Jesus steps from the ecstasy of Jordan River to the agony of wilderness. It's time to be tempted by the devil.

We've noticed already that Matthew likes to show how Jesus fulfills Israel's longings. So Jesus' forty days in the wilderness may parallel Israel's forty years in the wilderness after their own mountaintop experience at Mount

Sinai (Exodus 19–20). After God gave Moses Israel's new way of life there, they learned in the wilderness to rely on God to supply their daily bread and to lead them to the promised land.

Forty days of fasting leaves Jesus "famished," so the devil says: make yourself some bread from stones. Seems innocent enough. Jesus will one day feed five thousand people from seven loaves. But this is about reliance: as Israel waited for manna, so Jesus must wait for God to feed him. He won't live by bread alone, but by every word from God's mouth.

Even Jesus faced temptation

• Jesus uses Scripture to answer temptation. What helps you resist when you are tempted?

• What do you think it means to "live by" the Word of God? What doesn't it mean?

Another temptation: "Throw yourself down. God will save you." We can see the diabolic logic. "Let's take that reliance on God out for a spin, shall we?" But Jesus will have none of it. Don't test God! Jesus answers.

Finally, the devil offers the whole world. "All these I will give you, if you will fall down and worship me." To this Jesus offers the centerpiece of Israelite faith: "Worship the Lord your God, and serve only him" (Matthew 4:10; compare Deuteronomy 6:4-9). Irony abounds here. This one will himself be properly worshiped (Matthew 8:1-2; 9:8; 14:33; 28:16). But first there is work to do.

Jesus' temptations don't end here. In Caesarea Philippi, the voice will be Peter's: "This must never happen to you," to which Jesus will reply, "Get behind me, Satan!" (Matthew 16:23). In the Garden of Gethsemane, hours before torture and crucifixion, Jesus will hear it again, "Let this cup pass from me," but the answer will be resolute: "Not what I want but what you want" (Matthew 26:39)

Jesus' staying power, forged in the wilderness, becomes our salvation.

Background Files

The Historical John. The Jewish historian Josephus writes:

"Now many people came in crowds to John, for they were greatly moved by his words. Herod, who feared that the great influence John had over the masses might put them into his power and enable him to raise a rebellion (for they seemed ready to do anything he should advise), thought it best to put him to death" (*Antiquities* 18.119).

Gospel Sources. Matthew and Luke present Jesus' temptations with similar detail, but Mark does not (Mark 1:12-13). Since the two obviously use the Gospel of Mark for other parts of their story, scholars have asked how they came to share content that is not in Mark. Three hypotheses work: Matthew read Luke before writing; Luke read Matthew before writing; or they both knew another source that we no longer have. Scholars call this hypothetical source "Q" (for the German word for *source, quelle*).

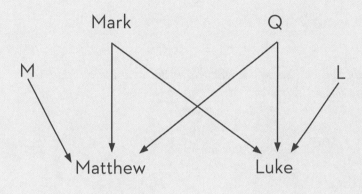

PICTURING THE STORY

As you watch the story unfold in the video, consider:

- What did the artist help you see in a new way?
- What do you find most remarkable or intriguing in the stories surrounding the baptism and temptation of Jesus?
- What questions are raised for you?
- If you could ask John the Baptist a question, what would it be?
- Do you see Jesus in a new way? If so, how?

SINGING THE STORY

Just as the Psalms were the songbook of the people of Israel, so Christians have written and sung hymns and songs to convey the story of Jesus and its meaning.

"Prepare Ye the Way of the Lord" (Stephen Schwartz)

Prepare ye the way of the Lord!

A single, repeated line echoing the words of John the Baptist (Mark 1:3) begins the musical *Godspell*, by Stephen Schwartz. John himself was echoing the words of the ancient prophet Isaiah (40:3). How has the way to Jesus been prepared for you? Is anything still blocking the path?

MARK IT

Choose one or more of the following passages to read during the coming week. Mark your readings using the marking method shown below.

Luke 4:12-13   John 3:16-21
Hebrews 4:14-16   Romans 6:1-11

Marking Your Bible

Make notes about the questions and insights you have as you read your Bible. The following symbols might be helpful.

∗ A chapter or verse important to me
! A new idea
√ A passage to memorize
? Something not clear to me
∞ God's love
ⓟ A promise from God
≈ Something that connects with my experience
† My relationship with God
↔ My relationships with others

Next Time

Use the following suggestions to prepare for Session 4.

Read the following passages and review study notes in *Lutheran Study Bible* from:
- Matthew 4:12-17, 23-25
- Mark 1:14—2:12
- Luke 4:14-44
- John 2:1—3:36

Gospels Reading Plan

If you wish to read one entire Gospel or all four Gospels during the sixteen weeks of this study, follow this weekly reading plan.

Week 3: Matthew 4:12—5:48; Mark 2:1—3:35; Luke 4:14—5:39; John 4:1-54

4

FULFILLED IN YOUR HEARING
Ministry Begins

The Spirit of the Lord is upon me, because he has anointed me . . .

Who is Jesus? Over the course of two millennia, many and various answers have been offered. We've heard the four Gospel writers reply, in their introductions and in the words of their characters. Subsequent history has continued the question, and we don't always get the answer right. In skewed imaginations, the Prince of Peace has even been styled King of Crusaders and Inquisitor General.

Who is Jesus? Now, in a brilliant moment we lay aside commentary and encounter for the first time Jesus of Nazareth himself. And this is privileged access. Jesus does not usually tell us about himself. In sports parlance, he lets his game do the talking—as he will do casting out a demon in Capernaum and healing Peter's mother-in-law. But for a moment in a Nazareth synagogue, Jesus lets us in on what he tells a waiting crowd he's up to.

SMALL TOWN, BIG ASPIRATIONS (Luke 4:14-30)

The scene begins innocently enough. A hometown boy attends the synagogue of his youth and stands up to read Scripture. He asks for an Isaiah scroll and reads out the soaring words of chapter 61: "The Spirit of the Lord is upon me, because he has anointed me to bring good news to the poor" (Luke 4:18). Jesus continues, widening the glorious aid to captives, the blind, and the oppressed. A beautiful reading!

Afterward, Jesus hands the scroll to the attendant and sits back down. Presumably, custom called for comment, so the people wait expectantly to hear, "What the prophet is saying here . . .". All eyes are fixed on Jesus in silence. But instead of launching an interpretation, Jesus claims the words for himself. "Today this scripture has been fulfilled in your hearing" (4:21).

Jesus announces his mission

To be fair, the Nazarenes in the synagogue haven't been where we've been. They didn't stand by the river Jordan and watch as "the Holy Spirit descended . . . like a dove" (Luke 3:22); they didn't chew their nails as Jesus "was led by the Spirit in the wilderness" to be tempted by the devil (Luke 4:1-2); and they didn't breathe a sigh of relief as the undaunted Jesus returned to town "filled with the power of the Spirit" (Luke 4:14). When we hear "the Spirit of the Lord is upon me," we're warmed up for it. The people of Nazareth are not. What's more, they have not heard God's voice say, "You are my Son, the Beloved (Luke 3:22)." They only know him as Joseph's kid.

- Why is it sometimes hard to convince hometown friends and family to take you seriously? What has been your experience with this?

So Jesus' announcement confuses them. At first they are amazed. Maybe they pat his head, saying, "This is Joseph's son!" Whether they mean it proudly ("That's our boy!") or condescendingly ("What good can come of him?!"), Jesus takes issue. He compares himself with Elijah and Elisha, two spirit-filled miracle-working prophets from the Hebrew Scriptures.

The people respond violently. Jesus narrowly escapes being pushed off a cliff. Then he walks to the next town and begins preaching good news to the poor, release to captives, sight to the blind, and freedom to the oppressed.

- Are you surprised at the way Jesus is treated in his hometown synagogue? Why?

This time he talks with his hands.

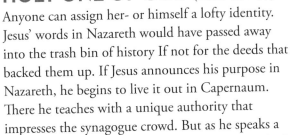

HOLY ONE OF GOD (Luke 4:31-37)

Anyone can assign her- or himself a lofty identity. Jesus' words in Nazareth would have passed away into the trash bin of history If not for the deeds that backed them up. If Jesus announces his purpose in Nazareth, he begins to live it out in Capernaum. There he teaches with a unique authority that impresses the synagogue crowd. But as he speaks a troubled man steps forward and raises a ruckus. It is then that Jesus embodies Isaiah 61, by healing a man's demon possession.

What could be more oppressive than the destructive presence of evil overwhelming a life? When Jesus encounters that, not only in Luke 4 but

- How are you a beneficiary of Jesus' work in your life?

throughout the Gospels, he confronts it directly—and ends it. Here, the demonic voice speaks defiant words: "Let us alone!" and then "I know who you are—the Holy One of God" (Luke 4:34). Jesus answers, as we might say it today, "Shut up, and come out of him!" And the demons simply do. The crowd marvels. "They were all amazed and kept saying to one another, 'What kind of utterance is this? For with authority and power he commands the unclean spirits, and out they come!'" (4:36)

This is a remarkable scene! Since the Enlightenment and the rise of science as an authority in Western culture, many have attempted to explain these phenomena without recourse to a spirit world, in terms of known maladies like epilepsy and mental illness. Others acknowledge the existence of a spiritual realm and picture the story as the narrator does. Still others imagine that some un-personified form of spiritual bondage is the explanation. We don't know what diagnosis a twenty-first century doctor or psychiatrist would render for the man in that Capernaum synagogue. What we do know is that, whatever plagues this man, Jesus has begun to let the oppressed go free.

- How is evil "cast out" in today's world?

If Jesus is still in the business of casting out demons, what in the world does it look like now?

HEALED AND GRATEFUL (Luke 4:38-41)

Walk into any prayer meeting in any church you know and listen to the requests people offer. "Please pray for my Aunt Linda. She has surgery next week to remove a lump." "Pray for my son, who has the flu."

Why do we think God cares about such things? The story of Jesus healing Simon's mother-in-law begins to answer that question. Such a mundane condition: she has a fever. We've all had one. We reach for the pain relievers. There's no mandate here to abandon modern medicine!

But Simon's wife's mom doesn't have Tylenol® as an option, and she's sick, so Jesus fixes it. He "rebukes" the fever and it stops. He'll do this for a lot of other people in the next couple of verses, healing various diseases and throwing out more demons. But this instance deserves our attention, because we get a comment about what happens afterward: "Immediately she got up and began to serve them" (4:39).

Jesus' healings do not require righteousness as a prerequisite. He seems to think it's enough to help paralytics walk, blind people see, bleeding people stop, dead people breathe. Jesus never stands over his beneficiaries and says, "All right, *quid pro quo.* Here's what you owe me."

Jesus heals people with no strings attached. But Simon's mother-in-law "got up and began to serve them" (Luke 4:39). Hers is one of the several times when Jesus' healing comes with an after-story. A healed leper sees his fresh skin and rejoins his faith community (Mark 1:40-45). Blind Bartimaeus receives his sight and immediately "followed [Jesus] on the way" (Mark 10:52). A demon-possessed man in Gerasa tells all his neighbors about the good man who made him whole (Luke 8:39). Only one of ten healed lepers comes back to Jesus and expresses his gratitude (Luke 17:11-19). After Jesus heals Joanna, Susanna, and Mary Magdalene of various infirmities, they support and follow him (Luke 8:1-3). There are others. These are grateful people, who direct their changed lives to the work Jesus has begun.

Jesus' work begins with a healing touch

- How do you relate to any of the groups Jesus came to help: the poor, the blind, the captives, or the oppressed?

- What shape has your gratitude taken? Now what?

- How has your changed life joined Jesus' work?

Background Files

A Lay Reader. In Luke 4, Jesus reads from the Scriptures in the synagogue. Unlike the temple in Jerusalem, where priests served exclusively and where the people were passive, synagogues welcomed the participation of the laity. Scripture was also uniquely important in the synagogue: "The centrality of the text in the synagogue's liturgical agenda was . . . revolutionary," says Lee I. Levine in *The Ancient Synagogue* (New Haven: Yale University Press, 2005, p. 3).

Ancient Exorcists. Jesus was not the only exorcist in antiquity, of course. Magic was a prevalent piece of life in ancient Rome—among both non-Jews and Jews. In a playful story from the first century, Rabbi Hanina ben Dosa casts a demon out of a woman who "suffers grief from the evil spirit." This story comes from the Talmud, a fourth-century collection of rabbinic sayings. The Apostle Paul encounters twelve itinerant Jewish exorcists in Ephesus, according to Acts 19.

Geography. Find Nazareth and Capernaum in Galilee on the map "Palestine in Jesus' Time," page 2109 in *Lutheran Study Bible*. Approximately how far apart are these cities?

PICTURING THE STORY

As you watch the story unfold in the video, consider:

- What did the artist help you see in a new way?
- What do you find most surprising or disturbing in these stories?
- What questions are raised for you?
- If you could ask one of the people a question about their encounter with Jesus, which person would it be? What would you want to know?
- How could you, or do you, participate in the mission Jesus has announced?

SINGING THE STORY

Just as the Psalms were the songbook of the people of Israel, so Christians have written and sung hymns and songs to convey the story of Jesus and its meaning.

"Will You Let Me Be Your Servant" (Richard Gillard, b. 1953)

Will you let me be your servant,
let me be as Christ to you?
Pray that I might have the grace
to let you be my servant, too.

We are pilgrims on a journey,
we are trav'lers on the road;
we are here to help each other
walk the mile and bear the load.

Reflect on Jesus' mission. How do Richard Gillard's words invite us into that mission? What roads do you travel? Does Jesus walk alongside?

MARK IT

Choose one or more of the following passages to read during the coming week. Mark your readings using the marking method shown below.

Mark 2:1-12   John 4:7-15
Romans 5:6-11   1 John 4:7-12

Marking Your Bible

Make notes about the questions and insights you have as you read your Bible. The following symbols might be helpful.

*   A chapter or verse important to me
!   A new idea
√   A passage to memorize
?   Something not clear to me
∞   God's love
Ⓟ   A promise from God
≈   Something that connects with my experience
†   My relationship with God
↔   My relationships with others

Next Time
Use the following suggestions to prepare for Session 5.

Read the following passages and review the study notes in *Lutheran Study Bible* for:
- Matthew 9:35—10:33
- Mark 2:13—3:35; 8:27—9:1
- Luke 5:1-11, 27-39; 6:1-16
- John 1:35-51; 8:21-59

Gospels Reading Plan
If you wish to read one entire Gospel or all four Gospels during the sixteen weeks of this study, follow this weekly reading plan.

Week 4: Matthew 6:1—7:29; Mark 4:1-41; Luke 6:1—7:50; John 5:1-47

5

FOLLOW ME
Calling Disciples

If any want to become my followers, let them deny themselves and take up their cross and follow me.

We all have established patterns of life. We have our places and our people and our routines. We aren't sure that ours is the right or the best way, but it's our way and we've gotten used to it. Anything that interrupts our way threatens us.

Jesus made a habit of interrupting established, routine lives and calling people out of them. "Follow me!" he said. And suddenly fishermen, tax collectors, and a whole lot of others stepped out of their familiar daily routines and into a whole new Way. They didn't know much about this new Way. Once they followed, these people discovered a life far more challenging and far larger than the one they lived before.

The Danish philosopher-theologian Søren Kierkegaard called this holy risk-taking a "leap of faith"—the willingness to jump out into the hands of God without absolute knowledge of what will happen next.

DEEPER WATERS (Luke 5:1-11)
Accountants don't tell surgeons where to cut. Surgeons don't tell artists how to balance a canvas. Artists don't tell businesspeople how to turn a profit. We humans don't take kindly to people telling us how to do what we think we're good at.

Peter is a fisherman. He's no throw-in-a-line-and-pull-out-a-beer sportsman. He lives by fishing, and people who live by fishing must learn where and when to put out nets. They have to know currents and recognize the sky's hints about what weather is next.

Peter is a fisherman who has just had a bad night. He caught nothing, and catching nothing matters. He has a family to feed. So Peter likely isn't cheery when a carpenter's son steps into his boat and starts teaching. And he gets downright defensive when that carpenter's son has the audacity to give him professional advice. Jesus recommends the deep water. Peter tries to stay calm, then says: "Master, we have worked all night long but have caught nothing. Yet if you say so . . ." (5:5). Can you hear the sarcasm?

Of course, Jesus is right about the deep waters. They catch enough fish to sink the boat, and Peter is undone. Seeing the astonishing haul "he fell down at Jesus' knees, saying, 'Go away from me, Lord, for I am a sinful man!'" (5:8).

What is Peter confessing? Here's a thought: Maybe before he can really follow Jesus, Peter has to learn that Jesus knows more about living than he does. Following Jesus will run Peter and all of us into a lot of these peculiar moments, when his commands seem imprudent or fruitless or even mistaken. He'll tell us it's better to give than to receive, better to turn the other cheek than to hit back, better to gain a soul, even if we lose the whole world.

In these moments, we'll notice our innate resistance. The chief question of our lives comes in these moments: Will we muddle on with a paltry catch? Or will we follow the carpenter's call to deeper waters?

Jesus calls some fishermen

- What do you think of the comment that Jesus knows more about living than we do? What does this mean to you?

- Which appeals to you more— standing in the shallows or heading into deeper waters? Why?

PHOTO OPS AND TROPHY WALLS (Luke 5:27-32; Matthew 9:9-13)

Just think what Jesus could have done if he had hired a public relations consultant. Jesus must have been compelling and charismatic, because people thronged to see his wonders and hear his words. But his strategy was all wrong. Presidential campaigns and the trophy walls of movers and shakers teach us that the key to winning is finding the right photo op. Being caught on camera with the right people in the right places is crucial to popularity.

In this scene, Jesus sits down to dinner with the Syrian mafia. Levi, the tax collector, has just pledged to follow Jesus and wants to celebrate with a feast.

Jesus calls tax collectors and eats with sinners

- What would it mean for you to take on Jesus' habit of making friends in low places?
- Who do you hang out with?

Of course, the people of Galilee loathed tax collectors. These "revenuers" made their living defrauding their neighbors, and the people were helpless to oppose them. What's not to hate? So Jesus accepts Levi's invitation and parties with a whole stable of these disreputable taxmen. There were other sinners, and Jesus eats with them too. This is political suicide! Couldn't Jesus kiss a baby? Visit a senior center? Bowl with the commoners?

Jesus loves people others despise. He hangs out with "tax collectors and sinners," not as social rebellion or niche marketing, but because they matter to God and because they need God. When others question his dinner company—as they do often—he answers that healthy people don't need a doctor, sick people do! (5:31).

Imagine this trophy wall. There's no photo of Jesus at a fund-raiser with Herod, or at a party with the chief priests. Instead there's a snapshot of Jesus standing with a leper. Another has him down in the dust speaking kindly to an adulterous woman. In one he even has his arm around a known political dissident. And here's a photo of Jesus with a tableful of tax collectors.

These photo moments are not prudent choices. But they seem to be what Jesus meant when he said, "The kingdom of heaven has come near" (Matthew 3:2; 4:17; 10:7).

So what's on your trophy wall?

DISCERNMENT (Luke 6:12-16)

How do you make big decisions? When we choose our careers or our life partners, when we buy big-ticket items like houses and cars, we hope to pause long enough to think carefully. Discernment in the big matters of life is a big deal. What are your criteria? What is your preparation?

Despite his questionable choice of friends, Jesus' popularity somehow grew exponentially. The Gospels picture him crushed by crowds, unable to move freely, forced to teach from a boat to accommodate the masses. In this wide slice of humanity, the level of commitment to Jesus' work must have run the spectrum from curiosity-seeking to deep devotion.

Jesus knew how fleeting popularity can be. In fact, he told parables that pictured plants that sprout up promisingly but soon wither, likening them to early enthusiasm that won't endure. When Jesus decided it was time to choose an inner circle of followers, he sought a devoted few. He would teach them and mold them; he would also expect much of them. These would be his disciples. He wanted twelve.

Luke doesn't outline Jesus' process. Does he write a pros-and-cons list for each candidate? Does he check references? What criteria does he apply to his decision? We don't know the answer to any of these questions. Maybe he just knew it like you know a good melon.

What we do know is that, faced with a huge decision, Jesus prayed. As Luke puts it, "He went out to the mountain to pray; and he spent the night in prayer to God. And when day came, he called his disciples and chose twelve of them." How did that night of prayer go? Again, we don't have details. But have you ever spent a whole night in prayer? Jesus was convinced that his big decisions required it.

Jesus rose from prayer and called the twelve

- For you, what role does prayer play in making decisions—no matter the size?

- What does Jesus' call to "follow me" look like now that he is not walking the earth? What would make a person say "Yes!" to that call?

REDEFINING MESSIAH
(Mark 8:31-36)
Question: Who is Jesus? Answer: Messiah. God's anointed one. The long-awaited king from the line of David.

Peter's answer is right. But once the title has been named, Jesus immediately begins to redefine what Messiah means. The people Israel have for centuries longed for a powerful military-political conqueror to help them throw off Babylonian or Persian or Greek or Roman rule and lead them into a new era of independent self-rule in their land. Some of Jesus' followers have already written this script for him. They imagine him as the king and themselves prominent in the king's court (Mark 10:35-37).

In this scene, Jesus rewrites both his script and theirs. His destiny will not be military or political conquest of the oppressors. To the contrary! Instead, he will suffer and die at the hands of those very oppressors. It must have been shocking for these Messiah-followers to hear. And worse yet, in Jesus' script his followers would not seek position or glory, but would carry their own crosses—would even give up their lives. It's no wonder that Peter "rebuked" Jesus. "Lord, no! You've got it all wrong!"

Jesus' reply startles us: "Get behind me, Satan!" (Mark 8:33). In these harsh words to Peter, we can hear Jesus reckoning with the pressing temptation to ascend, to pursue our own ends, to "gain the whole world." We hear in it echoes of the time Jesus was offered the whole world by Satan in the wilderness. "All these I will give you if you will fall down and worship me" (Matthew 4:9).

What does Jesus demand of those who would follow? In Dietrich Bonhoeffer's words, "Jesus bids us to come and die." The Apostle Paul called this ever-dying devotion a "living sacrifice" (Romans 12:1). Jesus raises for us an urgent question: What does this dying look like in your life and mine?

Background Files

Tax Collectors. These men were extremely unpopular in Jesus' time, because they were most often Jews who it was thought had "sold out" to the Roman overlords. They made their money by charging more than Rome required and keeping the margin for themselves.

Messiah. This term literally means "anointed one." The word was used to describe priests and kings of Israel, and even Cyrus of Persia—anyone God designated for a specific task. After Babylonian armies ended King David's dynasty, which many believed would last forever (2 Samuel 7:16), some Jews began to use this term to describe a coming military-political redeemer from David's lineage who would return Israel to self-rule.

Getting the Call. Luke's calling of the disciples differs from Matthew's (4:18-22) and Mark's (1:16-20), where Jesus seems to "cold call" Peter and Andrew and James and John, without any prior acquaintance. As usual, John's account is quite different from the other three (1:35-51).

PICTURING THE STORY

As you watch the story unfold in the video, consider:

- What did the artist help you see in a new way about the call of the disciples?
- What, if any, questions are raised for you?
- Which disciple would you most like to ask about his initial encounter with Jesus? How do you think you would react if Jesus suddenly appeared and said, "Follow me"?
- What do you think the cross of Jesus feels like?

SINGING THE STORY

Just as the Psalms were the songbook of the people of Israel, so Christians have written and sung hymns and songs to convey the story of Jesus and its meaning.

"Will You Come and Follow Me" (John L. Bell, b. 1949)

Will you come and follow me if I but call your name?
Will you go where you don't know and never be the same?
Will you let my love be shown, will you let my name be known,
Will you let my life be grown in you and you in me?

Imagine Jesus speaking Bell's words to you. How will you answer? What do you think of the prospect of going to unknown places or having your life never be the same?

MARK IT

Choose one or more of the following passages to read during the coming week. Mark your readings using the marking method shown below.

Luke 5:9-11   John 7:25-31
Ephesians 4:1-6   Romans 10:14-17

Marking Your Bible

Make notes about the questions and insights you have as you read your Bible. The following symbols might be helpful.

* A chapter or verse important to me
! A new idea
√ A passage to memorize
? Something not clear to me
∞ God's love
℗ A promise from God
≈ Something that connects with my experience
† My relationship with God
↔ My relationships with others

Next Time
Use the following suggestions to prepare for Session 6.

Read the following passages and review the study notes in *Lutheran Study Bible* for:
- Matthew 8:23-27; 14:1-21
- Mark 4:35-41; 6:35-44
- Luke 8:22-25; 9:10-17
- John 4:46-54; 6:1-21

Gospels Reading Plan
If you wish to read one entire Gospel or all four Gospels during the sixteen weeks of this study, follow this weekly reading plan.

Week 5: Matthew 8:1—9:38; Mark 5:1-43; Luke 8:1-56; John 6:1—7:52

WHO THEN IS THIS?
Making Miracles

6

Who then is this, that even the wind and the sea obey him?

We spend a lot of our time sizing people up. A supervisor at work, a spouse, a stranger in church, a potential friend—all require interpretation. Who is he? Who is she? We may not put our question in those words, but we sure ask it, and we answer by looking at the things these mysterious others do.

Understandably, the people around Jesus ask the "Who is he?!" question a lot, because Jesus' power makes him a very mysterious other. When they see him do wonders—like transforming water into fine wine, calming a storm, feeding a lot of people with a little bread, and even raising a man from death—they can't find a category that fits him. They try on names from their religious past, like "Son of Man" and "Son of God" and "Messiah," but none of them are quite adequate.

Let's ask with them: "Who then is this?"

STORMY WEATHER (Luke 8:22-25)
We haven't yet talked about the comedy of Scripture—the sheer humor of some stories that shake us out of our "sacred text" mode and make us laugh out loud.

As the dangerous storm raged, the hero slept. That line has comic potential. We picture the disciples frantically bailing water, viciously tossed around by the sails, shouting loud instructions, desperately working to keep the creaky old boat afloat. And in the stern, their fearless leader—whose idea it was to sail today in the first place!?—naps.

CHAPTER 6: WHO THEN IS THIS? ● 45

Jesus calms a storm

- When has God calmed a storm in your life? When has God *not* calmed a storm in your life?

When the storm gets the best of them, they wake Jesus: "Master, Master, we are perishing!" (8:24). You and I probably read their words as a cry for help, but are they? Are the disciples confident that Jesus can fix this? Or are they waking him up so he can know that he is going down with the ship?

Luke isn't absolutely clear on this. But a minute later Jesus will chide: "Where's your faith?" Why would he say this if they woke him trusting that he could solve the problem? Wouldn't that demonstrate their faith? This seems to fit more with their customary unbelief. The famous scene where Jesus feeds the five thousand (see below) is followed shortly by a reprise, this time with four thousand hungry people. But instead of trusting that Jesus can supply, the disciples panic: Where are we going to get all that food (Mark 8:4)?

- Why would you wake up Jesus?

Are the disciples doing that here? Are they forgetting Jesus' power? "Sure, he has cast out demons, healed all kinds of diseases and made a paralyzed man walk. But can he really calm a storm?" Is it gallows humor, as they imagine all is lost when there's a storm-stilling power right there with them?

It seems so. The disciples seem surprised when he pulls it off: "Who then is this, that he commands even the winds and the water, and they obey him?" We want to shout the answer. They seem so clueless! Then, after a moment of comic reflection, humility returns and we wonder who might want to shout the answer to us amidst the storms of our lives.

BREAD FOR THE WORLD (John 6:5-15)

"Six months' wages would not buy enough bread for each of them to get a little." These are Philip's words to Jesus in the face of five thousand hungry people on a hillside. Jesus has "tested" him by asking, "Where are we to buy bread for these people to eat?" Andrew is also flummoxed. The total food inventory is one boy's lunch, consisting of five loaves and two fish. Andrew's question: "But what are they among so many people?"

What follows is the famous subject of churchy children's books. The little boy gives Jesus his lunch, and soon the whole crowd is full up, with left-overs. The Sunday school moral of this story: give what you have to Jesus, and Jesus will do great things. It's a good moral, as morals go, but it's not the one this crowd draws.

Mark makes this feeding a pretext for showing that once again the disciples just don't get it. It's fine when they are surprised that he feeds five thousand people. But then, two chapters later, four thousand unfed people show up and the disciples are at a loss: "How can one feed these people with bread here in the desert?" (Mark 8:4). Moral: Remember the good God does for you and expect great things. Another good one, but not what this crowd is thinking.

The people in John 6 wonder who could do such wondrous things, so they search their possible answers and say, "This is indeed the prophet who is to come into the world" (6:14). They look at Jesus and see that the long-awaited prophet like Moses (see John 6:32) has arrived.

The people are close. Jesus doesn't correct them here. But down three paragraphs he'll talk again of feeding them. It turns out that Jesus is not just the bread-maker. He is "the bread of God . . . which comes down from heaven and gives life to the world" (John 6:33).

It's a good thing to look for a moral. But sometimes it's best for us to leave aside how we should be or what we should do and just marvel: "Who is this?!"

Jesus feeds the five thousand

- Can you think of times in your life when you have slipped like the disciples do about the storm and the bread? Have you experienced great things from God one time, and then panicked the next?

- Does Jesus want to feed hungry people in our world? How can the multiplication of food happen today?

STRANGE GRAVESIDE MANNER (John 11:1-44)

Once one of Jesus' friends gets really sick, the kind of sick when doctors tell you, "Hurry to the bedside." But Jesus gets delayed. It happens. People get delayed. But when your friend's really sick, who knows how long you've got? Who knows about people who are really sick?

Jesus gets delayed, Lazarus dies, and everyone cries. Sister Mary cries. Sister Martha cries. And then even Jesus weeps. Their brother is dead. His friend is dead. To the people in the neighborhood, the scene looks pretty normal. A loved one dies. Friends and family gather to grieve.

But then it suddenly isn't normal at all. Jesus tells someone to remove the stone from the tomb's door. "Lazarus, come out!" Those are Jesus' words.

And at first onlookers must feel sorry for him. He misses his friend. It's normal. Maybe he's deranged? Or is he joking? If he's joking, none of us think it's funny! The crowd is just debating whether Jesus has a loose screw or a sick sense of humor when something . . . moves. With death clothes still clinging to him, Lazarus sticks his head out his stinking tomb.

"The last enemy is death," Paul writes. And indeed it is. Disciples panicking in a storm-tossed boat fear death. Hungry crowds who have stayed too long with the teacher fear it too. It is deeply built in us to fear death. It's one of the reasons our sort have survived all these hundreds of thousands of years.

But in this story of Lazarus, Jesus tells us that not even death gets the last word with him. "I am the resurrection and the life" (John 11:25), he says. Jesus can't mean that he will save us all from dying. Lazarus will die again. No, this life points to another life. And so, three chapters later, in John 14:1-7, Jesus will speak assurance to his bewildered and fearful disciples: "In my Father's house there are many dwelling places. . . . I go to prepare a place for you."

Who then is this that even death can't stop him?

Jesus raises Lazarus from death

- How does it matter for your picture of God that when he heard that Lazarus had died, "Jesus began to weep" (John 11:35)?
- Jesus did not heal every sick person, calm every storm, feed every crowd, raise every dead friend. What do the times that he did these things mean to you? Is God arbitrary?

Background Files

Miracles. Through the centuries, people have asked whether Jesus really did the miracles the Gospels report. Some believe that they happened as described. Others naturalize the miracles (for example, Jesus could walk on the Sea of Galilee because he knew where the rocks were). Others count the miracles as myth—story intended to characterize Jesus, but not historical. Austin Farrer, a mid-twentieth-century commentator on Mark's Gospel, was asked by skeptics, "Do you really think all these wild stories you discuss are true?" Farrer replied, "I don't know that. But this I do know: God is the only author who can write with history."

Old Testament Precedents. In Exodus, Moses parts the Red Sea (Exodus 14) and calls on God to provide bread (called "manna") for Israel in the wilderness (Exodus 16:31). The prophets Elijah and Elisha, whom we met in Session 4, are both credited with miraculously raising someone from the dead (1 Kings 17:17-24; 2 Kings 4:17-37).

PICTURING THE STORY

As you watch the story unfold in the video, consider:

- What did the artist help you see in a new way about Jesus' miracle-working?
- What, if any, questions are raised for you?
- Think of the various people touched by Jesus' miraculous power in these stories. What would you want to ask anyone who witnessed Jesus in action?
- Have you ever experienced what you would call a "miracle"?
- What miracles are needed in the world today?

SINGING THE STORY

Just as the Psalms were the songbook of the people of Israel, so Christians have written and sung hymns and songs to convey the story of Jesus and its meaning.

"It Is Well with My Soul" (Horatio Spafford, 1828–1888)

When peace like a river attendeth my way,
when sorrows like sea billows roll,
whatever my lot, thou hast taught me to say,
It is well, it is well with my soul.

Refrain

It is well with my soul,
It is well, it is well with my soul.

How does Jesus help you ride life's waves? When have you most felt that "it is well" with you?

MARK IT

Choose one or more of the following passages to read during the coming week. Mark your readings using the marking method shown below.

1 Kings 17:17-24   1 Corinthians 15:12-22
1 Corinthians 11:23-26   John 6:35-40

Marking Your Bible

Make notes about the questions and insights you have as you read your Bible. The following symbols might be helpful.

* A chapter or verse important to me
! A new idea
√ A passage to memorize
? Something not clear to me
∞ God's love
℗ A promise from God
≈ Something that connects with my experience
† My relationship with God
↔ My relationships with others

Next Time
Use the following suggestions to prepare for Session 7.

Read the following passages and review the study notes in Lutheran Study Bible for:
- Matthew 8:1-17; 9:27-33; 20:29-34
- Mark 5:1-43; 1:40-45; 10:46-52
- Luke 5:17-26; 17:11-19; 18:35-43
- John 5:1-9; 9:1-41

Gospels Reading Plan
If you wish to read one entire Gospel or all four Gospels during the sixteen weeks of this study, follow this weekly reading plan.

Week 6: Matthew 10:1—11:30; Mark 6:1-56; Luke 9:1-62; John 8:1-59

WHO TOUCHED ME?
Healing

Daughter, your faith has made you well.

Great power is not necessarily good. As world history and any decent fantasy novel will attest, power may be exercised for good or for ill. Consider God and Satan, Gandhi and Hitler, Aslan and the White Witch, Dumbledore and Voldemort. Experience and poetry both tell us that power is neutral until directed.

A part of what is compelling about Jesus is the compassionate way he directs his power. The Gerasene demoniac, the woman who can't stop a flow of blood, and a well-to-do man's sick little twelve-year-old girl are very different characters. They all have dire need. And Jesus answers their need with healing power.

How can we latter-day disciples of Jesus follow in these steps? Not many of us can exorcise demons, heal sick people, or raise the dead. At that great gift we can only marvel. Compassion, on the other hand, is ours for the taking.

VACATION INTERRUPTED (Mark 5:1-20)

This guy was scary! He lived in the graveyard because no one wanted him in town. In Luke's version, he's been homeless and naked for a long time. I picture him foaming at the mouth. He has the kind of dangerous strength and chaotic unpredictability that terrifies people. He breaks through chains and shackles. He even beats himself up. Imagine not even being harmless when you're alone. Most of us only see such things in movies.

Jesus is coming off a long day. He just preached to thousands along the Capernaum shoreline—so many people that he had to launch a boat into the shallows so people could see and hear him (Mark 4:1). After all that, he was tired enough to sleep through a storm. He may even be headed for Gerasa to get away for a retreat and prayer. He does that sometimes.

Jesus calls out demons

- Do you see demons in your world? What do they look like? If not, what is it that is demonizing this man?

This destruction machine meets Jesus at the shore. It turns out that his scary strength comes from demons. Destructive power has come to battle divine power. So much for retreat. "We are legion!" they cry out to Jesus, and, like other demons, they know right away that they're dealing with the "Son of the Most High God" (5:7).

The scene turns comic with the dialogue—"Don't send us out of the country." "Okay, how about into the pigs?"—but the overall picture is poignant. Jesus' tranquil, anonymous landing at Gerasa is cataclysmically interrupted by a violent, troubled man. But Jesus does not row away, as some of us might do. Instead, he faces the man's demons straight on and says, "Come out of the man, you unclean spirit!"

- Have you ever fought something harmful in yourself that is too strong for you to get rid of? What was or is it? What was—or is—your plan?

As Jesus prepares to leave town, the grateful, no-longer-destroying man meets him at the boat and asks if he may accompany Jesus. But Jesus has other work for him. The man listens, then begins to "proclaim . . . how much Jesus had done for him; and everyone was amazed." Can you picture this man, for the first time in his life, welcomed?

HEALING TOUCHES (Mark 5:21-43)

Have you ever been "better-offered" at a party? You're in the middle of a conversation with someone when his or her eyes look past you, over your shoulder, at someone who is, at least in the moment, more important than you. A quick brush-off follows, and you are left looking for the hors d'oeuvre tray. This does not feel good.

The rest of Mark 5 is a "better-offer" scenario turned upside down.

First, we need information we don't have yet. The first phase of Jesus' ministry in Mark has featured two main sociological developments: the exponential growth of Jesus' popularity and growing tension between Jesus and the Jewish leaders. As the crowds get bigger, the leaders get feistier, in what begins to look like turf defense. Five times in two chapters, they challenge Jesus—over who can forgive sins, whether holy people should feast or fast, what one can do on the Sabbath, and, ultimately, where he gets his power—from God or the devil. The intensity of the Jewish leaders' hostility is captured in Mark 3:1-6, where a Sabbath skirmish ends with Pharisees plotting Jesus' demise.

When our passage begins with "one of the leaders of the synagogue" approaching Jesus, it looks like same song, sixth verse. But instead of ranting at Jesus, Jairus asks for help. His little girl is really sick. He's desperate. Could Jesus please come and heal her?

The disciples surely do a double take. Some of them may have worried that all those arguments with the Pharisees were burning bridges they'd like to keep. This looks promising. Maybe if Jesus helps Jairus, maybe Jairus will help Jesus. They practically push Jesus forward.

So Jesus sets off for Jairus's house. But as they weave through the crowds that always surrounded Jesus, the good teacher suddenly pulls up as if hurt. "Who touched my clothes?" (5:30) he asks, and the whole mass of humanity stops. The disciples can't believe it. "Five hundred people have touched you, Jesus. Now let's go!" But Jesus insists and waits, until finally a disheveled woman leans in, embarrassed, and confesses: "I'm the one. I touched you, and now I'm well."

That could have been enough. She's fine, or at least her body is. He could have jumped right back on that path to the little girl. But Jesus listens. As Jairus squirms nervously and the disciples wait impatiently, the woman tells Jesus how she'd been bleeding mysteriously for twelve years; how of course you can't go near polite society when you're bleeding, because Israel's holy law says so (Leviticus 15:19-31); how the doctors tried everything and failed. She's a talker, this one, and the meter is running, but Jesus just listens. There are bigger fish to fry. But Jesus listens. We can picture Peter muttering under his breath: "C'mon Jesus! She's healed already!" But Mark says he hears "the whole truth." When she finally stops, he says, "Your faith has made you well!" (Mark 5:34)

Jesus heals Jairus's daughter and the woman with a hemorrhage

- In what character(s) do you most easily see yourself in these stories? The hemorrhaging woman? Jairus? Jesus? The disciples? The little girl? Why?

Bad news finds Jairus just as Jesus is finishing. "It's no use," say his servants. "Your daughter is dead." But Jesus presses on. "Only sleeping," he says, and his determined steps quicken. From the woman who's been disabled for twelve years, he moves to a girl who has only lived for twelve years. "Show me to her room." The servants scoff. The household mourns. "Talitha cum," Jesus says—meaning "Little girl, get up!" And suddenly she sits up. Jesus' next words break the tension: Can somebody get her a snack?

- What need would make you rush to Jesus for help?

Jesus seems to look over the shoulder for a *worse* offer. He risks an advantageous relationship to linger with a nobody, probably for the simple reason that no one else will linger with her.

- How do you make decisions about how and with whom to spend your time? As God continues to build your life, how has that changed or how might it change?

And there's another layer of compassion, if we look for it. After seeing nothing but the backside of the synagogues' hand for weeks and months—knowing, probably, that Jewish leaders are already plotting his demise (see Mark 3:6)—Jesus doesn't hesitate when a leader of the synagogue asks him for help. "All is forgiven. Where is she?"

"Jesus, Thou art all compassion! Pure, unbounded love Thou art," wrote Charles Wesley in on of his best hymns. Maybe he was reading Mark 5.

PICTURING THE STORY

As you watch the story unfold in the video, consider:

- What did the artist help you see in a new way?
- What do you find most interesting in these stories? Is there something you want to know more about?
- What questions are raised for you?
- If you could ask anyone in these stories a question, which person would it be? What would you want to know?
- Jesus heals in these stories. What else does he do? What might this say about being a follower of Jesus?

SINGING THE STORY

Just as the Psalms were the songbook of the people of Israel, so Christians have written and sung hymns and songs to convey the story of Jesus and its meaning.

"There Is a Balm in Gilead" (African-American spiritual)

Refrain
There is a balm in Gilead
to make the wounded whole;
There is a balm in Gilead
to heal the sin-sick soul.

Sometimes I feel discouraged
and think my work's in vain,
but then the Holy Spirit

revives my soul again.
Refrain

If you cannot preach like Peter,
if you cannot pray like Paul,
you can tell the love of Jesus
and say, "He died for all."
Refrain

How is Jesus healing balm for you? For others? Healing comes in many ways. How can words convey healing? Which words?

MARK IT

Choose one or more of the following passages to read during the coming week. Mark your readings using the marking method shown below.

Mark 3:1-6	Acts 3:1-10
Luke 17:11-19	Hebrews 11:1

Marking Your Bible

Make notes about the questions and insights you have as you read your Bible. The following symbols might be helpful.

*   A chapter or verse important to me
!   A new idea
✓   A passage to memorize
?   Something not clear to me
∞   God's love
℗   A promise from God
≈   Something that connects with my experience
†   My relationship with God
↔   My relationships with others

Next Time

Use the following suggestions to prepare for Session 8.

Read the following passages and review the study notes in *Lutheran Study Bible* for:
- Matthew 5:43-48; 18:15-35
- Mark 2:1-12
- Luke 6:27-36; 7:36-50; 19:1-10
- John 8:1-11

Gospels Reading Plan

If you wish to read one entire Gospel or all four Gospels during the sixteen weeks of this study, follow this weekly reading plan.

Week 7: Matthew 12:1-50; Mark 7:1-37; Luke 10:1—11:54; John 9:1—10:21

8

LET THE FORGIVEN FORGIVE

Forgiving

I forgave you all that debt because you pleaded with me. Should you not have had mercy . . . ?

Around the world every Sunday, Christians pray a very dangerous line in the Lord's Prayer: "Forgive us . . . as we forgive . . ." Most of us would be better off just asking God to forgive us, because our track record for forgiving others is spotty at best. We more likely fume and hold a grudge; or fake forgiveness while we secretly keep score. That doesn't bode well for folks who have just asked God to forgive us the way we forgive others.

Forgiveness is at the heart of Jesus' teaching. He wants people reconciled. When Peter asks Jesus how many times he ought to forgive a brother or sister, Jesus answers with the equivalent of infinity. Jesus forgives us, and he requires us to forgive others. No easy task, to be sure.

FORGIVENESS WITHOUT LIMITS

(Matthew 18:21-35)

You know the feeling: the same person has let you down over and over. How long do you have to put up with this? How much is enough?

It's a simple question: "How many times?" The rabbis of Jesus' day discussed this often. "How many times must a person forgive?" Some said three. Others said seven. Peter had sensed that Jesus might be on the generous side of this conversation, so he asked, "As many as seven times?" Jesus moves the conversation out of the range of the rabbinic debate and toward infinity: "Seventy-seven times"—and that Greek phrase is sometimes translated as "seventy times seven" (see the NRSV note).

Before Peter can express his astonishment, Jesus tells a story. A master loaned an astronomical sum of money to one of his servants—10,000 talents, or 150,000 years' wages for a laborer. The man could not pay the loan back on time. So he fell on his knees and begged, "Have patience with me, and I will pay you everything" (18:26). The master gave the guy a break.

So the man left, relieved, but when he saw a fellow servant who owed him a couple bucks, he demanded repayment—even when the poor guy pleaded for extra time. How's that for a short memory?! For a few bucks, the guy with the big debt throws the guy with the little debt in prison.

Things don't go well for the unforgiving servant. The master finds him and subjects him to torture until he can pay the debt in full. Next come some of Jesus' most chilling words: "So my heavenly Father will also do to every one of you, if you do not forgive your brother or sister from your heart" (Matthew 18:35).

Jesus' picture of God is rough. Many of our preachers hope to coax us into forgiving others: "Come on, you'll feel better if you forgive." Jesus doesn't seem concerned about that. We scoff at the ridiculous ingratitude of the unforgiving servant, not because he misses a chance for self-satisfaction, but because he is unjust. Jesus wants us to scoff. And then he wants us to realize the injustice of our own failure to forgive. The Apostle Paul captures Jesus' simple call: "Forgive each other; just as the Lord has forgiven you, so you also must forgive" (Colossians 3:13).

Jesus speaks of forgiveness

- Why does Jesus want us to forgive those who wrong us? Why do you forgive?

- How do you know when you've finally forgiven someone?

- What danger is there in forgiving without limits?

YOU WANT ME TO LOVE WHO?! (Luke 6:27-36)

Retaliation is big with us humans. "Eye for eye, tooth for tooth," says Moses' law (Leviticus 24:19-21; Deuteronomy 19:16-21), and we can feel our DNA cheering.

But Jesus stops us up short again with an outlandish expectation. He doesn't just tell us to forgive our friends. He wants us to love our enemies. He wants us to be kind to those who hate us. If someone hits our cheek, we should turn to offer the other. If someone takes our coat, we should say, "Take my shirt too."

This is problematic, because we have revenge in us and we like our stuff. Jesus here seems utterly impractical. To help us see the forest in which these tall trees stand, Jesus groups all these strange acts under love. He gets us to admit that it's pretty easy to love people who love us and lend to those who will pay us back. But a God-like love goes farther. God is kind to the ungrateful and the wicked, and, as Matthew's Jesus says, "makes his sun rise on the evil and the good" (Matthew 5:45). Jesus says the apple shouldn't fall far from the tree. If that's the way God loves, that's the way God's children ought to love.

Of course, the Son himself will, in time, show us what this family resemblance looks like. After Peter denies Jesus three times (Matthew 26:69-75; John 18:15-27), Jesus will not only forgive him but even send him out to feed his flock (John 21:15-19) and love the world in his name (Matthew 28:16-20). When enemies beat him and flog him and put him up on a cross, and even scoff as he hangs there, Jesus will look their hatred in the eye and say, "Father, forgive them; for they know not what they are doing" (Luke 23:34).

The deeds match the words with this Christ. He forgives, and he loves in the face of hatred. He's so inspiring that some part of us might even begin to hope that he can form in us his very problematic, impractical love.

Love your enemies!

- Love our enemies goes too far, doesn't it? It leads to abuse and oppression, right? How can you understand Jesus' clear directive to love your enemies?

- Who is the hardest person in your life for you to love? Why? How will God help you?

TO ERR IS HUMAN . . . (Luke 7:36-50)

The source of our hope to forgive and to love our enemies is the astonishing, forgiving love of God. Jesus radiates that amazing love.

A sinner walks into a Pharisee's house. That fact alone is enough to make this story compelling. (Imagine a porn star boldly taking her place in the front pew or getting in line to receive the Lord's Supper.) But she walks, carrying an alabaster jar full of ointment. We don't know what kind of "sinner" she was, but the people around the table likely did. The silence in the room is deafening.

What the woman does next—right there at the dinner table—can't help. She falls to the floor, bathes Jesus' feet with her tears, dries them with her hair, kissing them, and rubs ointment on them. Any time Jesus meets with

Pharisees, he is on trial, and this helps their case. Simon, the host, mutters under his breath that if Jesus were a prophet, he would know "that she is a sinner."

Little does Simon know that Jesus now has him right where he wants him. First, he tells a story about two people who owe money: One owes fifty denarii, the other ten times that much. Neither can pay, but the creditor forgives both men their debt. Which one will be more grateful? Who knows whether Simon is on to Jesus by now, but, if so, he plays along: "I suppose the one for whom he canceled the greater debt."

The trap is set. Jesus tells how Simon offered Jesus none of the customary signs of hospitality—no water and towel for his feet, no kiss of greeting, no oil for his head. But this woman has bathed, dried, and kissed and anointed Jesus' feet. Why? She is forgiven much, so she loves much. Simon, who thinks he needs little forgiveness, loves little.

It's a nice lesson, but the elephant in the room is Jesus' presumption. When Jesus forgives sins, the Jewish leaders get the willies. When he forgives a paralytic man in Mark, they ask, "Who can forgive sins but God alone?" (Mark 2:1-12). When Jesus forgives the woman with the alabaster jar, they simply size him up: "Who is this who even forgives sins?" (Luke 7:49)

Alexander Pope said, "To err is human; to forgive, divine." Jesus and his critics both agree with Pope. They just disagree on who is divine.

Your sins are forgiven!

- When you try to forgive, how does it help that Jesus has already forgiven you?

- Is there anything God can't forgive?

Background Files

Rabbinic Context. If you search the Internet for *rabbis* and *forgiveness* and *Matthew 18* you'll get a bucketful of Christian sermons and papers that claim the rabbis unanimously said that forgiving someone three times was enough. The problem with this is that the rabbis never all agree on anything. This question was a live one for the rabbis, and they debated it, just as they did all other matters of Torah. But Jesus' answer to Peter lies outside the scale of that debate.

Luke and Generosity. In Luke 6, Jesus tells his disciples, "Give to everyone who begs from you; and if anyone takes away your goods, do not ask for them again." Luke, more than the other Gospels, displays the radical generosity of Jesus' vision. His John the Baptist tells the repentant what their new life should look like: "Whoever has two coats must share with anyone who has none; and whoever has food must do likewise" (Luke 3:11).

PICTURING THE STORY

As you watch the stories unfold in the video, consider:

- What scene most captures your imagination? Why?
- What new or surprising thing do you notice or feel?
- What questions are raised for you?
- Imagine that you are one of the people in these stories. What is going on in your mind or your emotions?
- How would you say that forgiveness and love are connected?

SINGING THE STORY

Just as the Psalms were the songbook of the people of Israel, so Christians have written and sung hymns and songs to convey the story of Jesus and its meaning.

"The Lord's Prayer"

Our Father . . .

Jesus' prayer (Matthew 6:9-13; Luke 11:2-4) has been set to music in a number of ways and with varying texts. Choose one to listen to or sing. How do you hear the words differently when they are sung? What is both simple and profound about this prayer?

MARK IT

Choose one or more of the following passages to read during the coming week. Mark your readings using the marking method shown below.

Luke 7:49	1 Corinthians 13:4-7
Romans 13:8-10	Colossians 3:12-17

Marking Your Bible

Make notes about the questions and insights you have as you read your Bible. The following symbols might be helpful.

*   A chapter or verse important to me

!   A new idea

√   A passage to memorize

?   Something not clear to me

∞   God's love

Ⓟ   A promise from God

≈   Something that connects with my experience

†   My relationship with God

↔   My relationships with others

Next Time

Use the following suggestions to prepare for Session 9.

Review the study notes in *Lutheran Study Bible* for:
- Matthew 5:1—7:29
- Mark 7:1-23
- Luke 6:17-26
- John 14:1-31

Read the following passages from the Gospels:
- Matthew 5:1—7:29
- Mark 7:1-23
- Luke 6:17-26; 11:1-13
- John 12:37-50; 14:1-31

Gospels Reading Plan

If you wish to read one entire Gospel or all four Gospels during the sixteen weeks of this study, follow this weekly reading plan.

Week 8: Matthew 13:1-58; Mark 8:1—9:1; Luke 12:1-59; John 10:22—11:57

9 BLESSED ARE YOU
Teaching

You are the light of the world. A city built on a hill cannot be hid.

Jesus' Sermon on the Mount has turned worlds upside down. It inspired St. Francis of Assisi to live simply with his brothers on Italian hillsides amidst medieval church opulence; it laid the pattern for Mahatma Gandhi's non-violent liberation movement in India; and it led the way for Martin Luther King Junior's peaceful demonstrations that turned the tide of American race relations. And then there are all the quietly heroic saints who have lived this Sermon-on-the-Mount life unrecognized by history.

The power of this sermon in history is a bit surprising, given that history books are full of military conquests and political maneuvers. The Sermon on the Mount paints a peculiar new way to live in the world. In it, Jesus blesses the least likely, moves the external demands of Moses's law into the depths of our souls, trades in showy religion for faithfulness with integrity, and calls all people everywhere to rely on God rather than wealth.

A STRANGE REVOLUTION (Matthew 5:1-12)

When Jesus opens his mouth to teach for the first time in Matthew's Gospel, expectations are already high. The prologue has dubbed him the Messiah (1:1); a genealogy has traced his lineage to the mighty King David (1:2-17); wise men from the east have inquired where the new king would be born (2:1-12); taking no risks, Herod has massacred all the infants to eliminate his competition (2:16-18); and John the Baptist has pictured the Messiah bringing fiery judgment to the earth (3:11-12). These images of power stack one on the other here, and as if all that weren't enough, Jesus climbs a mountain to deliver this sermon *à la* Moses.

The first words of this one who would be powerful king and righteous judge? "Blessed are the poor in spirit . . . those who mourn . . . the meek . . .

the peacemakers . . . those who are persecuted." Soon to come will be "do not resist an evildoer" and "love your enemies." Those who thought heads would roll are disappointed. No armed revolution, this.

The Greek word translated "blessed" here is *makarios* (Latin *beati*, and so the title "Beatitudes"). It means a special kind of "happy." For Homer it was the blissful state of the gods, with leisure and no toil. For Aristotle it began to describe the rich, who were similarly unperturbed by work and other worldly concerns.

Here Jesus does a strange thing: he names the very people who should be most un-happy on the toil-versus-leisure scale *makarioi*—really happy.

Do the Beatitudes console or command? Does Jesus speak them to surprise and gratify people who don't know they are God-blessed? Or does he want all of us to become "poor in spirit . . . meek . . . merciful," and so on?

What if it's both? The Revised Common Lectionary—the three-year schedule of Bible readings for worship—lists the Beatitudes each year on All Saints Day. On the one hand, the Beatitudes celebrate saints who have aligned their lives with this high call; on the other hand they assure us that God will care for all the blessed throughout eternity.

Jesus teaches the Beatitudes in his Sermon on the Mount

- Do you find yourself among the blessed? Do you want to be? Why?

- What person or persons do you consider blessed? Why?

- If you hear Jesus' blessings as partly prescriptive, how can you become more "pure in heart," more of a "peacemaker"? Can we make ourselves "hunger and thirst for righteousness"?

LET THERE BE LIGHT
(Matthew 5:13-16)

At least as strange as the Beatitudes' blessings are Jesus' next words, where he tells his ramshackle bunch of fishermen and tax collectors that they're crucial in the big world. They are "the salt of the earth" and "the light of the world." We can be pretty sure that no one had called them that before.

For most of us, salt has exhausted its significance once we have seasoned our food. Maybe it keeps our icy roads less slick. But in Bible times its uses were various and significant. Salt not only seasoned food but was crucial to preserving it. Moses's law commands that salt be included with Israel's sacrifices (see Exodus 30:35; Leviticus 2:13; Ezra 6:9; and Ezekiel 43:24). Symbolically, salt was used in making a friendship covenant (Numbers

You are light and salt in the world

- Think of people or churches who have been "light of the world" to you. What did they do or say that made it so?

18:19 and 2 Chronicles 13:5). Parents rubbed salt on newborn babies for health purposes (Ezekiel 16:4). Given all these ways that salt mattered in ancient lives, Jesus may as well say, "You are central to the world's well-being!"

- Jesus does not say "become the light of the world"; he says "you are . . ." How are you the light of the world right now?

In our time and place, light is everywhere. Cities stay lit all night, and we can illuminate most anything by the flick of a switch. Ancients could not, of course. All they had for light was flame. Darkness was a greater threat, and light therefore more cherished. "You are the light of the world" makes a huge claim about these disciples. They are a shining "city built on a hill." Paraphrased, Jesus says, "The whole world will get its bearings from you."

Jesus adds a concern to each claim: the prospect that salt could lose its saltiness or that light might be hid under a bushel. For Jesus' disciples, for Matthew's congregation, and for us, there will always be a temptation to shrink back from the role Jesus gives us in the world. Following so close on the heels of two blessings on the persecuted (Matthew 5:10-12) Jesus' words bolster those ancient fearful-faithful ones, and they bolster all of us with strong encouragement not to turn back when discipleship stops being popular.

- What dark corners of our world most need light?

DAILY BREAD (Matthew 6:5-15)

The Lord's Prayer is surely the most-spoken and -memorized part of the Bible. Christians worldwide speak it together in weekly worship. But it is also dangerous. If familiarity hasn't bred contempt, it at least threatens to domesticate the powerful words of the prayer.

Here God is "Father." That's old hat to us who pray it often, but it was rare (some say new) among ancient faithful peoples. Kings were sometimes called "sons of God." But two chapters after God calls Jesus "my Son, the Beloved" at his baptism, Jesus lets us all into the family circle.

"Your kingdom come, your will be done." What would the world look like if this prayer "took"? Jesus would become normal. Everyone would do as he does, love as he loves. Imagine.

We pray that God will provide "daily bread," which really stands for all the things we need for daily living. But then we spend our time worrying about how we'll get our needs met. The line recalls the manna God provided Israel day by day in the wilderness. Asking for "daily bread" mindfully offers us the hope that we will actually feel our true reliance on God.

The most risky line in the prayer comes next. "Forgive us . . ." is a normal thing to ask God; but "as we also have forgiven" ratchets up the demand. Are we really praying that God will forgive us at the rate we forgive? In Matthew 18, Jesus will return to this in a parable about an ungrateful servant, whose master forgives him a huge debt, but who can't forgive the little bit an acquaintance owes him (see Session 8). Jesus requires people who pray this prayer to forgive.

In chapter 4 Jesus was "tempted by the devil" in the wilderness. It's no wonder he here adds "do not bring us to the time of trial, but rescue us from the evil one." Faith tests may produce endurance (James 1:2-3), but they are no fun. Jesus would spare his friends that torment.

That's the Lord's Prayer. Christians who would venture to pray these words earnestly and expectantly should beware. If God answered fully and immediately, the world as we know it would disappear.

Jesus' prayer

- Jesus teaches both what to pray and how to go about praying. How would you summarize his teaching?

- What would you say is the relationship between prayer and action?

- Which part or petition of the Lord's Prayer is most challenging for you?

WHICH MASTER WILL YOU SERVE? (Matthew 6:19-21, 24-34)

Is it unfaithful to have a 401K? Does saving for the kids' college tuition upset Jesus? Does faithfulness require living day-to-day, paycheck to paycheck? These questions hardly ever get asked from pulpits, but Jesus' words raise them.

"Do not store up for yourselves treasures on earth," Jesus says. They won't last. And not much later he supplies a second reason: "No one can serve two masters. . . . You cannot serve God and wealth" (6:24). In a paragraph or so, Jesus will add a third rationale: because the desire for material things makes us anxious.

It's striking that Jesus doesn't here lecture the moneyed for not helping the poor. He will in other places. Here, though, Jesus seems most concerned about us. Money will rule you. Money will make you anxious. Get rid of

- We tend to seek more money and save our money to eliminate anxiety. Do you think Jesus is right when he teaches that a desire for material things actually has the opposite effect?

- What worries do you have about today? Tomorrow? What does Jesus invite you to do with these worries?

it! Jesus pictures life that is better—not just morally better, but happier—without excess things.

How then shall we live? Some Christians through the ages and in the present have interpreted Jesus' call radically. St. Francis of Assisi took these words to heart and "married Lady Poverty." But most have hoped to understand Jesus and appropriate these words in a more "normal" day-to-day life. Quaker author Richard Foster's book title, *The Freedom of Simplicity*, captures this theme. He imagines building a life free from the anxieties and enthrallments of the material, so that it can be free for God.

Of course the history of Christianity and our own lives are loaded down with unscrupulous affluence. Once Søren Kierkegaard sat in a church in Copenhagen, surrounded by the gilded sanctuary with velvet pew cushions and ornate stained-glass windows. As the minister, garbed in fine linens, read out this passage from Matthew 6, Kierkegaard looked around and found, to his astonishment, that no one was laughing.

Background Files

"Blessed are . . ." Matthew's Beatitudes are different than Luke's (Luke 6:20-26). Where Matthew has "poor in spirit," Luke has "poor." Matthew's Jesus blesses those who "hunger and thirst for righteousness;" Luke's, those who are "hungry now." Most scholars imagine that both draw on the same source (Q). They disagree on whose version is nearer the original.

Light of the World. In Matthew, Jesus calls his disciples "the light of the world." In John, Jesus calls himself "the light of the world." The two statements are complementary. Christians exist as moons to Jesus' sun: in our better moments, we reflect the rays of heaven.

Daily Bread. Very few words in Scripture appear only once in all the ancient Greek texts. The Greek word *epiousion* (translated "daily") is one of them. Daily is an educated-guess translation, based on the story of manna in Exodus.

PICTURING THE STORY

As you watch the action unfold in the video, consider:

- Who is the best teacher you have ever seen or heard? What made her or him so good?
- What is it that makes Jesus a compelling teacher?
- What questions do Jesus' teachings raise for you?
- How bright is the light of Christ reflecting off you?
- How much worry in the world is related to money—getting it, keeping it, or letting it go? Why does Jesus say you cannot serve God and money?

SINGING THE STORY

Just as the Psalms were the songbook of the people of Israel, so Christians have written and sung hymns and songs to convey the story of Jesus and its meaning.

"This Little Light of Mine" (African American spiritual)

This little light of mine, I'm goin'a let it shine;
this little light of mine, I'm goin'a let it shine;
this little light of mine, I'm goin'a let it shine,
let it shine, let it shine, let it shine.

Jesus gave it to me, I'm goin'a let it shine;
Jesus gave it to me, I'm goin'a let it shine;
Jesus gave it to me, I'm goin'a let it shine,
let it shine, let it shine, let it shine.

How does the light of Jesus shine in you? Through you?

MARK IT

Choose one or more of the following passages to read during the coming week. Mark your readings using the marking method shown below.

Luke 6:20-26	1 Timothy 6:6-10
John 14:27	Philippians 4:4-7

Marking Your Bible

Make notes about the questions and insights you have as you read your Bible. The following symbols might be helpful.

* A chapter or verse important to me
! A new idea
√ A passage to memorize
? Something not clear to me
∞ God's love
Ⓟ A promise from God
≈ Something that connects with my experience
† My relationship with God
↔ My relationships with others

Next Time

Use the following suggestions to prepare for Session 10.

Review the study notes in *Lutheran Study Bible* for:
- Matthew 13:1-50
- Mark 3:19b—4:34
- Luke 8:4-15; 10:25-37; 16:19-31

Read the following passages from the Gospels:
- Matthew 13:1-8, 18-23; 22:1-14
- Mark 4:3-8, 14-20, 26-29
- Luke 8:5-15; 10:29-37; 16:19-31

Gospels Reading Plan

If you wish to read one entire Gospel or all four Gospels during the sixteen weeks of this study, follow this weekly reading plan.

Week 9: Matthew 14:1—15:39; Mark 9:2-50; Luke 13:1—14:35; John 12:1-50

THE KINGDOM IS LIKE . . . 10
Storytelling

And who is my neighbor?

Do you ever feel like the world is too much with you? Wouldn't you love a better alternative? An early summary of Jesus' preaching has him telling people, "The kingdom of God has come near" (Mark 1:15). But what does this kingdom look like? To paint that picture, Jesus often uses parables, stories that go where propositional teaching can't. A tiny mustard seed grows up to be a big bush, a little yeast raises the whole lump of dough, a man sells everything to buy a field and the great pearl that's buried there. The kingdom of God is like that, says Jesus.

Jesus tells kingdom stories called parables

- What makes stories memorable? Will your answer also be true for the parables of Jesus?

So what is the kingdom of God like now? Stories are timeless. Seeds then are seeds now; yeast then is yeast now. The parables of Jesus continue to capture faithful imaginations to this day.

THE OVER-ZEALOUS SOWER (Luke 8:4-15)
A parable can be great without being a great story. The parable of the sower is a good example. It is not a great story in the classic sense. Its character list—sower, seed, soil, birds, thorns, and other menaces—leaves a bit to be desired. The action isn't scintillating either. Watching paint dry seems exciting next to watching seeds grow.

If the plot of this parable has a cousin, it could be the film *Sliding Doors*, in which Helen makes a crucial decision, then the movie tracks both the *either* and the *or* of the outcome. Is that what Jesus is doing with the soils? Could be. Trouble is, in this parable no character, except perhaps the sower, makes a decision. Earth does not decide to be rocky or thorny or good. It just is some of those things.

- What is the main point of this kingdom story for you? If you were trying to communicate that point to friends now, what image would you use?

- Has God been like this sower in your life? Has anyone else been like this sower to you?

- What do you need to sow?

What does Jesus want from us here? It seems we're supposed to be the soil, and maybe that we should aspire to be good soil; but earth can't change itself. Does Jesus want us to feel helpless? Here's a thought: Jesus is a rock star by the time he speaks this parable. Crowds are flocking to him, and the question must eventually arise: are all these people going to stick around? Or are some fair-weather friends? Jesus may tell this parable to teach his disciples how this seed-spreading business goes: you win some, you lose some. Just keep throwing.

That brings us to the farmer. This is no seed miser. He throws seed on rocks and into sticker bushes. He'd probably toss a little on the hood of a car, into the middle of a lake, and onto a busy city street. This is one reckless sower. Seems like he'll do anything, go anywhere, risk any disappointment just to get a little real growth.

The kingdom of God is like that.

WHO IS MY NEIGHBOR? (Luke 10:25-37)

This parable is a *great* story. (It can happen, too.) An anonymous guy gets mugged and left to die. The first passerby seems promising: a religious leader. But, maybe because he shouldn't soil his priestly robes, he steps past. The second is a teacher of law. He knows all about helping the helpless—the law is full of that. But he also steps past. Odd.

The poor guy in the ditch must be doomed, because the next person on the scene is a Samaritan. The Gospel of John understates it: "Jews do not share things in common with Samaritans" (John 4:9). And this is a risky situation. Think of a black man finding a white girl hurt on the roadside in the United States in places where segregation and Jim Crow laws prevailed. Who's going to believe he found her that way?

Jesus' Jewish audience would surely jeer at the parable, expecting that if the Samaritan stopped, he might hurt the poor man worse. But surprise! The Samaritan steps up. He gives the half-dead man a ride to the inn, leaves him in good hands, and offers his credit card at the desk. "I'll check back in when I can." This Samaritan does everything right!

Great story, but why did Jesus tell it? Luke says a lawyer summoned it. "You shall love . . . your neighbor as yourself" is so vague. The lawyer wants to narrow the field of applicants and make his job a little easier, but Jesus won't do it. "And who is my neighbor?" the lawyer asks. "Which of these three, do you think, was a neighbor to the man?" (10:36), asks Jesus. When the lawyer grudgingly consents to the obvious, Jesus says: "Go and do likewise."

One other detail brings home Jesus' point. The only character in the story without an identity is the man who gets robbed. There's a team of robbers, a priest, a Levite, and a Samaritan. Then there is the unfortunate guy we just know as "a man." He is everyman and everywoman. If we, with the lawyer, are looking for a loophole, Jesus gives us none, only "Go and do likewise."

The kingdom of God is like that too.

The parable of the good Samaritan

- What keeps the religious folk from helping the half-dead man? Do you ever feel like them?

- The Samaritan's love is risky. Can you remember a time when yours was too? Describe that experience.

RICH MAN, POOR MAN
(Luke 16:19-31)

Jesus talks a lot about money, and Luke's Gospel focuses on what he says. It begins when Mary sings out her Magnificat (Luke 1:46-56); moves through the holy family's sacrifice of birds (2:24) rather than a lamb, a concession for the poor (Leviticus 12:8); then to Jesus' first beatitude: "Blessed are you who are poor" (Luke 6:20). The parables pick up this theme. We hear of a rich fool, who amasses and stores wealth, only to see an untimely death separate him from it (Luke 12:13-21). Soon a man who was "very rich" will decide not to follow Jesus when the demand is to "sell all that you own and distribute the money to the poor" (Luke 18:18-30).

Here, in chapter 16, Jesus tells about a "rich man" who was dressed in purple and daily "feasted sumptuously," but ignores poor Lazarus sitting at the end of his driveway. When they both die, Mary's Magnificat shows up again. Poor Lazarus takes his place in the bosom of Abraham, while the rich man goes, empty, away to Hades.

The story could end there. Its moral? Rich people must help poor people. But this rich man continues to be pathetic, ordering Lazarus around as if he doesn't notice that flames are licking at his own toes while the poor guy now

- Who is the Lazarus at your gate? What would it take to live your story away from this ending and toward a better one?

- Write your own parable to tell someone what you think the kingdom of God is like.

rests with the patriarch, Abraham. Can't Abraham order send Lazarus with water to cool the rich man's tongue, the latter asks. When Abraham says no, the rich man offers an alternative: send Lazarus to warn the rich man's brothers, lest they too end up in "this place of torment." Abraham refuses, declaring that people who didn't listen to Moses or the prophets won't be convinced "even if someone rises from the dead." Jesus' point: some people will never listen.

Jesus *doesn't* mean that rich people will never listen. The good news is that not all moneyed people flunk Jesus' test. Joanna, Mary Magdalene, and Susanna use their means to support Jesus and his disciples (Luke 8:1-3). The good Samaritan uses his money well (Luke 10), as does the father of the prodigal son (Luke 15:11-32). The rich chief tax collector Zacchaeus is the poster boy. He gives half of his money to the poor and plans to chase down everyone he has defrauded and repay them four times what they lost (Luke 19:1-10).

That's more like the Kingdom of God.

Stories about Farming. Jesus lived in an agriculture-based society. Subsistence farming was the main livelihood of the people in his crowds. In Newcastle, England, he would have talked about coal; in Silicon Valley, microchips. In Galilee it was farming.

Jerusalem to Jericho. With no police force, travel on ancient roads was notoriously dangerous, and this road was considered one of the worst.

The Hated Samaritan. Samaritan history began when Israel was conquered by the Assyrians in the seventh century B.C.E. The conquering power planted colonists to live among the Jews who remained in the land. Intermarriage was common. Among the Jews in the still-standing Southern Kingdom (Judah), a form of racism took shape and grew over the centuries.

Geography. Locate the region of Samaria and the town of Jericho on the map "Palestine in Jesus' Time," in *Lutheran Study Bible*, page 2109.

PICTURING THE STORY

As you watch the parables unfold in the video, consider:

- What are your favorite stories? Why?
- Why does Jesus use stories to teach the truth about God's kingdom?
- What questions do these stories raise for you?
- Where do you see yourself in these stories? Where do you see God?
- Who needs to hear these stories?

SINGING THE STORY

Just as the Psalms were the songbook of the people of Israel, so Christians have written and sung hymns and songs to convey the story of Jesus and its meaning.

"Seek Ye First" (Matthew 6:33, adapted)

Seek ye first the kingdom of God
and its righteousness,
and all these things shall be added unto you.
Allelu, alleluia.

How does God's kingdom seek you? Where can the kingdom of God be found?

MARK IT

Choose one or more of the following passages to read during the coming week. Mark your readings using the marking method shown below.

Luke 8:15   1 Corinthians 3:5-9
James 1:17-18   Romans 12:1-8

Marking Your Bible

Make notes about the questions and insights you have as you read your Bible. The following symbols might be helpful.

∗   A chapter or verse important to me
!   A new idea
√   A passage to memorize
?   Something not clear to me
∞   God's love
℗   A promise from God
≈   Something that connects with my experience
†   My relationship with God
↔   My relationships with others

Next Time
Use the following suggestions to prepare for Session 11.

Review the chart in *Lutheran Study Bible* called "Jesus' Ministry," pages 1601–1603. Note items you have read and studied. Note other items you may have missed.

Read the following passages from the Gospels:
• Matthew 25:1-30
• Mark 10:13-16
• Luke 15:1-32

Gospels Reading Plan
If you wish to read one entire Gospel or all four Gospels during the sixteen weeks of this study, follow this weekly reading plan.

Week 10: Matthew 16:1—17:27; Mark 10:1-52; Luke 15:1—16:31; John 13:1-38

LOST AND FOUND
Storytelling

11

"Get the fatted calf and kill it, and let us eat and celebrate; for this son of mine . . . was lost and is found!"

How do you choose your dinner companions? Jesus gave strange advice on this topic: "When you give . . . a dinner, do not invite your friends or your brothers or your relatives or rich neighbors, in case they may invite you in return, and you would be repaid. . . . Invite the poor, the crippled, the lame, and the blind. And you will be blessed, because they cannot repay you" (Luke 14:12-14).

Jesus hung out with disreputable people. All four Gospels tell us so. He befriended tax collectors and prostitutes and the like and for that made quite a name for himself among the proper religious folks. They "grumbled" and said, "This fellow welcomes sinners and eats with them" (Luke 15:1).

Why? Because they were lost. Jesus thinks that is reason enough. To clarify he tells stories about a sheep, and a coin, and a boy. He wants to make sure everyone knows the disposition of heaven: God likes finding lost people.

SEARCHING FOR THE LOST (Luke 15:1-7)

Jesus appeals first to common sense. Any self-respecting shepherd with a hundred sheep who lost one would leave the ninety-nine and scour the hillsides 'til he found it. And upon return this shepherd would throw a party with his friends. A sheep is a dear thing to a shepherd. This lost one is now back in the fold.

The story of the happy shepherd is good on its own. The moral is straightforward: "There will be more joy in heaven over one sinner who repents than over ninety-nine righteous persons who need no repentance." The story gains power as we remember that somehow Jesus is the searching shepherd and the "sinners" around a dinner table with him are the lost sheep he hopes to find. They probably don't look so innocent as that—at least to us. But that's how Jesus sees them.

We don't normally look at the world that way. A popular contemporary Christian song prays, "Give me your eyes for just one second. Give me your eyes so I can see / Everything that I've been missing. Give me your love for humanity. / Give me your heart for the broken-hearted, the ones who are far beyond my reach. / Give me eyes for the long-forgotten. Give me your eyes so I can see."*

Oh, to have Jesus' eyes!

REJOICE! (Luke 15:8-10)

It's a coin. Jesus elsewhere tells his disciples not to become too enamored with coins. But here he is glad to celebrate a woman's reunion with hers. She has only ten, and one has gone missing, so she launches a house-scouring search. "What coin-losing woman wouldn't?" Jesus asks. And, like the shepherd who finds his sheep, the woman wakes the neighbors and launches a block party. "Rejoice with me," she shouts. "I found the coin that I had lost." Jesus' point is the same as with the sheep: "Just so, I tell you, there is joy in the presence of the angels of God over one sinner who repents."

Coins don't repent, of course—any more than sheep do. That's the limitation of this tale. It can show us heaven's party, but not exactly what started it. That's OK, though. Another parable is coming that many of us find even more powerful—and closer to home.

LET'S PARTY! (Luke 15:11-32)

The parable of the prodigal son is one of Jesus' most famous because it is one of his most powerful. It makes the parables about the sheep and the coin look like warm-up bands. Jesus is still on the subject of lost things, but the prodigal is a lost boy, which changes things. First, hardly anyone blames a sheep or coin for getting lost. But this son is blameworthy. Second, the shepherd and the woman have to go in search of their lost things, but the boy comes back on his own. Finally we get a lost one who actually has the capacity to turn around.

Both of these elements make for a more compelling story. We've moved out of the realm of common-sense analogy and into the place where real people live.

This son has offended all decent standards. He's drawn out the inheritance before his father is gone, and he spent the money badly. He has dishonored his father. A Bible translator in Guinea, West Africa, tells the story of testing his translation of this parable on Manika tribesmen, who are much closer to ancient Middle East culture than we are. They jeered when they heard about the son's actions, and they cheered and laughed when he found himself eating pig slop. The boy was getting what he deserved.

When they heard that the boy turns back home—on motives of self-preservation, mind you, and not sorrow for his deeds—the tribesmen readied themselves for his rightful comeuppance. Surely things would not go well for him at home.

But then the boy with the well-rehearsed speech gets to the end of the driveway, the father waiting on the porch sees him, and something strange happens: while the son is practicing his speech one last time, his father hikes up his tunic and sprints toward him. The son can't get words out before his father squeezes the breath out of him. Soon there will be a welcome-home party.

This ending is familiar to most of us, but the Manika men were shocked. With a mix of anger and longing they cried out: "What kind of father is this?!"

The parable of the prodigal and his brother

- Must we repent, change our minds, turn our lives around, before we can be found by God?

Like the Manika men, the older brother in the story can't fathom this. He's been faithful to his father, done all the work around the house, walked the straight and narrow, while pretty boy was living it up out on the town. Now look who gets the party? The malcontented, womanizing, irresponsible twerp, that's who. Older brother feels taken for granted. He cries injustice. And he has a point. But no one ever said the ne'er-do-well brother *deserved* a party. Apparently this story isn't about justice. It's about a father's love for his child.

And so our grumbling questioners—the ones who prompted Jesus to tell these stories in the first place (Luke 15:2)—reenter the scene. In a charitable characterization, Jesus has written them in through the character of the older brother. They have stayed home, and they have kept the covenant, while the company Jesus keeps has found every way to dishonor God. Their question is his: Why eat with sinners? Why party with the riff-raff?

• Do you resent the breaks that others may enjoy, even though they don't deserve it? What would it take for you to join in the celebration? What is the cost of self-righteous anger?

Poignantly, the father appeals to the elder son, rather than scolding him. He hopes to coax him into a new way of seeing his lost-and-found brother, hopes to coax him into the party. To the brother's angry questions, the old man offers the same answer as we heard in the sheep and coin stories (the lost is found; the dead lives); but this time we see heaven's rejoicing break out right before our eyes. The music is playing, the people are singing, the old man is out of breath from dancing. Will the older brother join in?

• What do you think these parables say about God's kingdom?

One of the most famous Christian hymns borrows from this story. "Amazing grace, how sweet the sound, that saved a wretch like me. I once was lost, but now am found; was blind but now I see."

What kind of father indeed!

PICTURING THE STORY

As you watch the parables unfold in the video, consider:

- What is the common theme running through each?
- With which character do you most identify? Why?
- What questions do these stories raise for you?
- Where do you see yourself in these stories? Where do you see God?
- Who needs to hear these stories?

SINGING THE STORY

Just as the Psalms were the songbook of the people of Israel, so Christians have written and sung hymns and songs to convey the story of Jesus and its meaning.

"Amazing Grace" (John Newton, 1725–1807)

Amazing grace!—how sweet the sound—
that saved a wretch like me!
I once was lost, but now am found;
was blind, but now I see.

Through many dangers, toils, and snares
I have already come;
'tis grace has brought me safe thus far,
and grace will lead me home.

How have you experienced John Newton's famous words? Where is "home" for you?

MARK IT

Choose one or more of the following passages to read during the coming week. Mark your readings using the marking method shown below.

Luke 15:7   Mark 1:14-15

Galatians 3:19-29   Psalm 51:1-12

Marking Your Bible

Make notes about the questions and insights you have as you read your Bible. The following symbols might be helpful.

* A chapter or verse important to me
! A new idea
√ A passage to memorize
? Something not clear to me
∞ God's love
℗ A promise from God
≈ Something that connects with my experience
† My relationship with God
↔ My relationships with others

Next Time
Use the following suggestions to prepare for Session 12.

Review the chart in *Lutheran Study Bible* called "Jesus' Ministry," pages 1601–1603. Pay particular attention to the list of parables. Are there some you would like to read that you may have missed?

Review the chart "The I AM sayings of Jesus in John's Gospel," in *Lutheran Study Bible*, p. 1773.

Read the following passages from the Gospels:

• John 6:22-59; 8:12-20; 10:1-21; 14:1-7; 15:1-17

Gospels Reading Plan
If you wish to read one entire Gospel or all four Gospels during the sixteen weeks of this study, follow this weekly reading plan.

Week 11: Matthew 18:1—19:30; Mark 11:1-33; Luke 17:1—18:43; John 14:1—15:27

I AM
Sayings and Symbols

12

Jesus said, "Before Abraham was, I am."

"What if God was one of us?" Joan Osborne's 1990's song title catches us, because we wonder with her. How can God be a human? And how can a human be God? John begins his Gospel by claiming that he's found the answer in a person. In Jesus, the Word of God—equal co-creator, God himself—became flesh and lived among us.

John's high claim about Jesus' identity has gotten him and his community in trouble. Some scholars have argued that certain stories in John reflect the fact that some were being excommunicated from the synagogue for their belief in Jesus (see John 9:22 and 12:42). They've lost their cultural place and some have lost their families because of this persecution. They've bet their lives on Jesus. If they are asking, "Is Jesus really who I think he is?" John has Jesus answer, "I am."

SOUL FOOD (John 6:25-59)
Father, I cry to thee for bread
With hungerd longing, eager prayer;
Thou hear'st, and givest me instead
More hunger and a half-despair.

George MacDonald's poem "Hunger" captures the heart's longing for God. Sometimes we misread our emptiness and try to fill it with material goods. Jesus knew people like us.

At the Passover Feast, the people ask Jesus why they should believe in him—what work should be a sign of his identity. They reference their ancient fathers and mothers, after that first Passover: "Our ancestors ate the manna

- Do you feel your need for God? Or do you know it intellectually? What form does your soul's hunger take?

- The people who hear Jesus call himself the bread of life think he is talking about material things. Do you ever find yourself feeling like spiritual truths whiz right past your ear? What helps you "get" them?

Jesus Is . . .

in the wilderness; as it is written, 'He gave them bread from heaven to eat'" (John 6:31). Instead of performing a sign, Jesus answers them with a direct word: God is giving you the true bread from heaven . . . "which comes down from heaven and gives life to the world" (John 6:32-33).

Like Nicodemus, who thinks that being born again means climbing back into his mother's womb (John 3:4), and the Samaritan woman at the well, who hopes that Jesus' living water will substitute for fetching at the well every day (John 4:15), these people think materially. "Sir, give us this bread always" (6:34).

Jesus answers more openly: "I am the bread of life. Whoever comes to me will never be hungry. . . . Your ancestors ate the manna in the wilderness, and they died. This is the bread that comes down from heaven, so that one may eat of it and not die. . . . And the bread that I will give for the life of the world is my flesh" (John 6:35, 49-51).

The people will have none of this. "Is not this Jesus, the son of Joseph? . . . How can he now say, 'I have come down from heaven'?" (6:42). The people are like we are sometimes with God: like two ships passing in the night. But then there are the times when the mystery of the Spirit becomes momentarily clear and MacDonald's words don't fit us anymore—when our soul tastes the bread of life and can't imagine ever being hungry again.

I AM . . . (select passages)

To those ancient Jewish Christians in John's house-church and to you and me, Jesus speaks frank mystery. The words are frank because they are simple. "I am . . ." cuts through guesswork and speculation. But Jesus is not speaking literally. He does not say, "I am a Nazarene prophet," or even, "I am God in the flesh." John does that. Jesus speaks in metaphors that help us picture the good God has for us in him. But they are metaphors, so there is mystery.

Jesus' good news at the Passover feast repeats itself in six more "I am . . ." moments in the pages of John's Gospel. The rest resemble the first. In each, Jesus reveals another aspect of God's character that is being displayed in him—usually in a setting that makes that specific aspect meaningful. Are you walking in darkness? Jesus is the light of the world (8:12; 9:1-11). Is your access to God blocked? Jesus is the gate (John 10:7, 9). Have you wandered away? The Good Shepherd will find you and care for you (John 10:11-18). Even death cannot undo you, because Jesus is the resurrection and the life (John 11:25-26). Need guidance? Jesus is the way, the truth, and the life (John 14:1-7). Feel unconnected to the source of your life? Jesus is the vine (John 15:1-17). These strong images are poetic invitations. They don't simply describe Jesus. They welcome us into his life. You may have noticed that one image rises above the rest. Jesus is "bread of life," "resurrection and life," and "way, truth, and life." "Life" is the only "I am . . ." that repeats itself, which makes good sense. In one of his only "mission statements," Jesus pronounces the reason for his time on earth: "I came that they might have life, and have it abundantly" (John 10:10). This life (Greek, *zoh-ay*) is "the light of all people" (John 1:4).

I am . . . Jesus . . . I am.

I REALLY AM! (John 8:48-59 and 18:1-11)

If we want to know who Jesus is, the "I am . . ." invitations are only a beginning. Twice in the Gospel of John Jesus drops an even larger claim, by saying simply, "I am." Jews ask Jesus why he's so mysterious about his birthday, and he says, "Before Abraham was, I am" (John 8:58). Then, when guards chase him down in the garden and ask if he's Jesus of Nazareth, he replies, "I am he" and they fall to the ground (John 18:5-6). Strange words, these!

As we make our way through the Gospels, we understand a lot simply as English readers. We see Jesus heal blind people, teach about lives of love, die on a cross, rise from the dead, and we get it. But some of what our ancient brothers and sisters wrote eludes us like code. Jesus' words "I am" are this way. How will Jewish skeptics understand them? Why do temple soldiers collapse when they hear them?

To understand these scenes, we need information we don't have. In Exodus 3, God calls Moses to lead the Hebrew people out of Egypt. Their conversation is one of the best-known of all Bible stories. It's not just a fun Sunday school scene. It opens the door for God's wondrous rescue. Soon God's

- Which of the "I am . . ." invitations of Jesus most reaches you? Why?
- What does it look like to accept the invitation?

- What other metaphors would you use to describe Jesus?

I really am!

- While first-century Jewish Christians probably "got it" right away, the use of "I am" here is subtle. How can you help yourself "get it" when Bible culture and language feels different than your own?

people will flee Egyptian oppression by walking right through a sea, eating bread from heaven, and drinking water that gushes from a rock.

When God calls Moses, he resists at first. "I'm not qualified." "I'm not your guy." But as he opens to the idea, Moses asks, "What if my Israelite brothers and sisters want to know who sent me?" God answers simply and mysteriously: "I AM WHO I AM" (Exodus 3:14). God is the great "I AM." Moses goes.

When Jesus says "I am" we have from his mouth what John said about him in the beginning: This is God in flesh. It's no wonder skeptics are perplexed and guards tumble to the ground. In these two moments, Jesus of Nazareth, Mary's son, a carpenter's boy, tells people that he was in on creation. Mystery indeed!

- Imagine knowing Jesus in Galilee and Jerusalem. How do you imagine yourself—as one questioning Jesus? As a soldier bowled over? As a follower drinking in Jesus' divinity?

- How do you complete this sentence for yourself? "I am _____."

PICTURING THE STORY

As you watch the video, consider:

- What images are most intriguing or compelling to you?
- How do metaphors or symbols help us understand the "truth" of something?
- What is most true for you about Jesus' "I am" sayings?
- Where do you see yourself in these stories? Where do you see God?
- Is there anything you wish Jesus would say about himself? If so, what?

SINGING THE STORY

Just as the Psalms were the songbook of the people of Israel, so Christians have written and sung hymns and songs to convey the story of Jesus and its meaning.

"Guide Me Ever, Great Redeemer" (William Williams, 1717–1791; tr. Peter Williams, 1722–1796, alt.)

Guide me ever, great Redeemer,
pilgrim through this barren land.
I am weak, but you are mighty;
hold me with your pow'rful hand.
Bread of heaven, bread of heaven,
feed me now and evermore,
feed me now and evermore.

How are you "fed" by the great "I am"? How does he guide you through this "barren land"?

MARK IT

Choose one or more of the following passages to read during the coming week. Mark your readings using the marking method shown below.

Exodus 3:1-15	Philippians 2:4-11
1 Peter 2:4-10	Revelation 5:6-14

Marking Your Bible

Make notes about the questions and insights you have as you read your Bible. The following symbols might be helpful.

- *   A chapter or verse important to me
- !   A new idea
- √   A passage to memorize
- ?   Something not clear to me
- ∞   God's love
- ℗   A promise from God
- ≈   Something that connects with my experience
- †   My relationship with God
- ↔   My relationships with others

Next Time
Use the following suggestions to prepare for Session 13.

Read the following passages and review the study notes in *Lutheran Study Bible* for:

- Matthew 21:1-45; 23:1—25:13
- Mark 11:1—13:37
- Luke 20:27—21:38
- John 12:1-50

Gospels Reading Plan
If you wish to read one entire Gospel or all four Gospels during the sixteen weeks of this study, follow this weekly reading plan.

Week 12: Matthew 20:1—21:45; Mark 12:1-44; Luke 19:1—20:47; John 16:1—17:26

ENTERING JERUSALEM

Holy Week

13

Blessed is the coming kingdom of our ancestor David!

As Jesus walks into Jerusalem, one era ends and another begins. There will be no miraculous healings in the city. His parables will move out of their blessed levity and trend strongly toward judgment. Things get serious in Jerusalem. Here Jesus will do what must be done, but it won't be fun.

Back in Galilee, Jesus grieved: "Jerusalem, Jerusalem, the city that kills the prophets and stones those who are sent to it! How often have I desired to gather your children together as a hen gathers her brood under her wings, and you were not willing! See, your house is left to you. And I tell you, you will not see me until the time comes when you say, 'Blessed is the one who comes in the name of the Lord'" (Luke 13:34-35).

As we open our Bibles today, we can see the sign: "Entering Jerusalem."

ENTER AT YOUR OWN RISK (Mark 11:1-11)

On the outskirts of Jerusalem, Jesus pauses to stage a show. This is odd for him. In all ways Jesus has been the opposite of show. He's taught his followers not to make a show of their religion and chastised hypocrites for making a show of theirs (Matthew 6:1-18). His ministry has been one spontaneous act of generosity after another. Here, though, he instructs his disciples: "Go into the village ahead of you, and immediately as you enter it, you will find tied there a colt that has never been ridden; untie it and bring it" (Mark 11:2). Jesus is not merely procuring transportation. He could walk to town in less time. Jesus is staging a show.

Why? Matthew supposes it is to fulfill prophecy (Matthew 21:4-5). In fact, he will awkwardly have Jesus ride two beasts at once, because he hears the

- Does Jesus enter Jerusalem with a purpose? If so, what might it be?

- Is there any place for such public displays by Christians in our time? What would be an example?

prophet require that. But for Mark and Luke there's no prophecy. Jesus just rides in on a donkey. It's what the crowd says and does that causes a stir.

The people throw palm branches down in front of Jesus and shout, "Hosanna!" It's a garden-variety expression of praise that appears only in this scene in all of Scripture. This is not newsworthy. Their next words are similarly unexceptional: "Blessed is the one who comes in the name of the Lord!" (Mark 11:9)

It's the words after those that will put Jesus on everybody's radar screen. Chief priests will discover it, and Roman intelligence men will take notice. There, on the outskirts of Jerusalem, where David reigned in Israel's heyday, where centuries of Jews have expected a Messiah to return, a crowd of worshipers raises its voice and shouts, "Blessed is the coming kingdom of our ancestor David!"

Right there on the outskirts of Jerusalem, the simple Galilean has staged a king's triumph. Now everyone is watching. What will Jesus do with their attention?

CLEANING HOUSE (Mark 11:12-19)

When Jesus walks in, the temple has been the sacred center of Israel's religion for nearly a thousand years, with only a century's interruption. That's how long it's been since priests first placed the Ark of the Covenant in the center of King Solomon's new building (1 Kings 8:6). Babylonian King Nebuchadnezzar probably thought he had extinguished Israel's religion when he burned it to the ground six hundred years back, but Ezra and Nehemiah rebuilt it, and the worship of Israel resumed. A tyrant called Antiochus Epiphanes profaned it with the paraphernalia of Greek gods two hundred years ago. But still the temple stands.

Jesus begins his week in Jerusalem at Israel's holiest site—and calls it unholy. He mourns the wide gap he sees between God's intention for the temple and the merchandise show in front of him. We don't know what Jesus saw there, but we may imagine it: Merchants holler out prices for their sacrificial animals, a commodity over which they exercise a monopoly. Money changers charge whatever fee they can get for their services. Jesus will have no barriers between the worshipers and their God.

All of this leads Jesus to do what prophets do: he acts out the truth. He drives out all the merchants and tosses the stands of the money-changers. He effectively blocks the whole economic operation of the temple. Then, to explain his actions, he shouts out the words of the prophet Isaiah: "Is it not written, 'My house shall be called a house of prayer for all the nations'? But you have made it a den of robbers" (Mark 11:17). It's no wonder that when the priests finally manage to arrest Jesus three days later, their first question will be about the temple.

At a comfortable reader's distance, it is too easy for us to make our own righteous shout, "Go get 'em Jesus!" Humility dictates a different question. After all, those Jerusalemites of old undoubtedly thought they were doing God's work as it should be done. It took Jesus' eyes to see what was askew. Christians in every age should ask, "What would Jesus throw down if he walked into my church?" "What would he say if he walked into my life?"

Jesus cleanses the temple

- Why did Jesus think he could rearrange temple furniture? What gave him the authority to say and do what he did in the temple?

- What would Jesus find unholy in our churches today? What would he tear down and toss out from your church? From your life?

APOCALYPSE NOW (Mark 13:1-37)

Jesus is most mysterious to us when he waxes apocalyptic, that is, when he talks about the end of time and his own return (13:26). Jesus pictures how God's angels will "gather his elect from the four winds" (13:27). Some twenty-first-century Christians anxiously anticipate this event, while others do not regard the end-times with the sort of urgent expectation that may have informed a first-century reading of the Gospels. Bumper stickers are created to capture the range of views: "In case of rapture, this car will be unoccupied," or, "In case of rapture, can I have your car?" All joking aside, Jesus expected his followers to be watchful, ready, and prepared.

Timing complicates things. Jesus spoke in the shadow of the temple (30 C.E.), but these words we read were written just before or just after a Roman army destroyed it (70 C.E.). In fact, scholars date the Gospels partly by how closely Jesus' predictions align with that actual Roman military maneuver. Mark vaguely expects the destruction: "Not one stone will be left here upon another; all will be thrown down" (13:2). Luke, on the other hand, pictures troops arrayed around the city of Jerusalem (Luke 21:20), as vividly as if he were reporting after the fact. How does that impact his story-telling?

Jesus predicts coming destruction and encourages followers to endure to the end

- Some first-century Christians thought Jesus would come back during their lifetimes. Some twenty-first-century Christians think the same in our time. What do you learn about such predictions from Jesus' teachings in Mark 13?

- Have you had "tribulations" in your life that required painful endurance? What helped you through them?

- Many people around the world live under oppression and with a persistent threat of death. How might Jesus' words produce endurance for them? And what about you? Have you ever sensed the urgency of coming destruction or death?

Complexity makes us focus on what we can know. Jesus clearly takes pains to prepare his disciples for times of distress. He tells them that they will be persecuted in both synagogues and Roman courts. The distress will split families, and they should expect to be hated. Under this pressure, Jesus places a high premium on endurance. But even in the face of these threats, they should not worry. God will be with them. "Say whatever is given you at that time, for it is not you who speak, but the Holy Spirit (Mark 13:11)."

This is hopeful. Jesus sees right through a wretched picture of oppression and domination to the God who will receive the faithful at the other end. And he doesn't expect his disciples to venture the difficult walk alone. He promises them God's presence in the Holy Spirit. Maybe this is where we find a word for us. Whatever the shape of our own tribulation and distress, Jesus' promise of God's presence in the Spirit reaches us too.

PICTURING THE STORY

As you watch the scenes of Jesus in Jerusalem consider:

- What images are most intriguing or compelling to you?
- Imagine that you are a spectator at one of these scenes. How do Jesus' actions surprise you? What would you want to ask Jesus?
- Imagine that you are a religious leader in Jerusalem. What worries you about what Jesus is doing and saying? What do you think should be done about it?
- Where do you see yourself in these stories? Where do you see God?

SINGING THE STORY

Just as the Psalms were the songbook of the people of Israel, so Christians have written and sung hymns and songs to convey the story of Jesus and its meaning.

"Ride On, King Jesus" (African American spiritual)

Refrain

Ride on, King Jesus, no one can hinder me.
Ride on, King Jesus, ride on, no one can hinder me.

King Jesus rides a milk-white horse, no one works like him,
the River Jord'n he did cross, no one works like him. Oh,

Refrain

I know that my redeemer lives, no one works like him,
and of his blessing freely gives, no one works like him. Oh,

Refrain

Where will you ride with Jesus? What rivers will you cross? Does he go to any place where we can't follow him?

MARK IT

Choose one or more of the following passages to read during the coming week. Mark your readings using the marking method shown below.

John 3:13-25	2 Timothy 4:6-8
Hebrews 10:26-39	Revelation 21:1-4

Marking Your Bible

Make notes about the questions and insights you have as you read your Bible. The following symbols might be helpful.

* A chapter or verse important to me
! A new idea
√ A passage to memorize
? Something not clear to me
∞ God's love
℗ A promise from God
≈ Something that connects with my experience
† My relationship with God
↔ My relationships with others

Next Time

Use the following suggestions to prepare for Session 14.

Read the following passages and review the study notes in *Lutheran Study Bible* for:
• Matthew 26:1-46
• Mark 14:1-42
• Luke 22:1-46
• John 13:1—17:26

Gospels Reading Plan

If you wish to read one entire Gospel or all four Gospels during the sixteen weeks of this study, follow this weekly reading plan.

Week 13: Matthew 22:1—23:39; Mark 13:1-37; Luke 21:1-38; John 18:1-40

BROKEN FOR YOU
Final Night

14

I will never again drink of the fruit of the vine until that day when I drink it new in the kingdom of God.

Jesus has been many things to his disciples. As teacher, he has shown them a brilliant new Way to live. As healer, he has made many whole. As leader, he has helped them begin to live his Way and heal others. Lately, he has been prophet, exposing hypocrisies among the leaders of the people.

Now the story turns. Now Jesus turns toward his own suffering. He prepares his disciples for it. He prepares himself for it. And, through the Gospels, he prepares us for it. The brilliant days of seaside sermons and rock-star crowds have passed. The music turns suddenly, inevitably, to a minor key. Our authors walk us into an upper room and a Last Supper, then to a garden for anguished prayer. Each tells it uniquely. All attest to its intensity. Ironically, Jesus' time has come.

TRAITOR IN OUR MIDST (Mark 14:1-2, 10-11)

Jesus has been supremely popular throughout his ministry. In Mark, he progresses quickly from lone itinerant (1:16-20), to local phenomenon (1:28, 45; 2:1, 12, 13), to regional celebrity (3:7-8). Popularity protects Jesus from his opponents. Early on, Jewish authorities plot his demise (3:6), but crowds always thwart their plans—even when he leaves his homeland of Galilee and goes to Jerusalem (12:12).

In our passage, "The chief priests and the scribes were looking for a way to arrest Jesus by stealth and kill him," but don't, fearing "a riot among the people'" (Mark 14:1-2). They need a way into Jesus' entourage. No wonder, then, that when "Judas Iscariot, who was one of the twelve, went to the chief priests in order to betray him to them . . . they were greatly pleased."

- Do you have any experience with fickle popularity? What would it have been like for Jesus to see the adoring masses turn?

- What do you think about Judas? Was he a pawn of the religious leaders? Was he tempted by the forces of darkness? Was he jealous of Jesus? Was he a thief? Or was he just playing a necessary and appointed role in the drama? Does it matter?

Jesus and his disciples share a final Passover meal

- What does it mean to you that Jesus' body was broken for you? That his blood was poured out for you?

The spy they've longed for shows up at their front door! The tide had turned.

The early Christians wondered how Judas could betray his Lord. Mark simply reports the action, but Luke and John imagine that Satan—the devil—enters Judas (Luke 22:3; John 13:2), and John demonizes Judas even further. In his story about the woman with the alabaster jar, Judas protests, "Why was this perfume not sold for three hundred denarii and the money given to the poor?" (John 12:4-5). John insists that Judas's motives are not pure. "He said this not because he cared about the poor, but because he was a thief; he kept the common purse and used to steal what was put into it" (John 12:6).

TABLE TALK (Mark 14:12-25)

We call that Passover meal the Last Supper, but it began as a feast. Jesus and his disciples arrange a room and gather to eat, because God rescued Israel from Pharaoh (Exodus 12). They are celebrating. And we know these disciples as "Saint Peter," "Saint John," and the rest, but they're young fishermen from the countryside, visiting the big city for the first time. Mark reminds us at the temple, when one of the disciples says: "Look, Teacher, what large stones and what large buildings!" (13:1). The city is full of pilgrims for the Passover Feast. The disciples must be giddy.

Mid-meal, Jesus changes the mood: "One of you will betray me." I imagine surprise and confusion. Jesus has told them three times already that he will be killed (Mark 8:31; 9:31; 10:33-34). But each time the disciples have resisted (8:32-33)—or been strangely unconcerned (9:30-34; 10:35-37). They've never quite gotten it. Here, solemnity descends. Is it Jesus' mood at the table that changes things? Each wonders aloud if he might be the traitor.

In this changed room, Jesus breaks bread. "This is my body." Soon after comes the cup. "This is my blood of the covenant, which is poured out for many." How did the disciples hear these words amidst that feast? For centuries priests of Israel have sacrificed a lamb at Passover. In another Gospel, when the Baptist first saw Jesus he blurted, "Look, here is the Lamb of God!" (John 1:36). Which dots did these disciples connect as Jesus spoke of

his body and blood? They once heard him say, "The Son of Man came
. . . to give his life a ransom for many" (Mark 10:45). How are they hearing
Jesus' words at the supper?

None of this has dented Peter's confidence. After supper, he is resolute:
"Even though all become deserters, I will not." Jesus returns grave foreboding: "Truly I tell you, this day, this very night, before the cock crows twice,
you will deny me three times" (Mark 14:29-30). Peter's loud protests will
not change the hard truth of human frailty.

• Poor Peter! When's the last time "pride goes before a fall" (see Proverbs 16:18) applied to you?

THY WILL BE DONE! (Mark 14:32-42)

It's human frailty that Jesus battles in the Garden of Gethsemane.

All of his ministry has been building toward the cross. Three times he has predicted it. But it is one thing to know suffering lies ahead. It is entirely another to face it when it arrives. No wonder Jesus is "deeply grieved, even to death" (14:34). Perhaps for the first time, on the eve of his crucifixion, he feels the full weight of his mission.

His prayer is intimate and honest. "Abba, Father . . . remove this cup from
me." The thought first occurred way back in Caesarea Philippi. Peter had
correctly called him "Messiah," and Jesus had just announced that this
Messiah would suffer and die. But Peter rebuked him, unable to imagine
that plight for God's Messiah. Jesus was tempted to agree: "Get behind
me, Satan! For you are setting your mind not on divine things but on
human things" (Mark 8:27-33). Now the temptation is more real. Luke
captures the intensity of Jesus' anguish: ". . . his sweat became like great
drops of blood falling down on the ground" (Luke 22:44). Like the
psalmists he has read since youth, Jesus cries out honestly to God:
"Remove this cup" (Mark 14:36).

Jesus prays in the Garden of Gethsemane

• When have you been driven to desperate prayer? What drove you there?

Then something changes in Jesus. Some of us have experienced anguished
prayer (though probably less so than this) and know the breaking point,
when our heart changes. Luke tells us that an angel strengthens him
(22:43). Maybe Jesus remembers his own words. He had taught his disciples

to pray "Your Kingdom come . . . Your will be done" (Matthew 6:10). In the face of his own suffering, he prays those words here: "Not what I want, but what you want" (Mark 14:36).

• How would your prayer life be different if you always prayed, "Not what I want, but what you want"?

The anguish of Jesus at Gethsemane is extreme. But anything less might have given him less access to us. The writer of Hebrews later pondered Jesus' anguish: "Because he himself was tested by what he suffered, he is able to help those who are being tested" (Hebrews 2:18). What Frederick Buechner said of the manger is true here as well: "Once you have seen God [there] you can never be sure where He will appear or to what lengths He will go or to what ludicrous depths of self-humiliation He will descend in His wild pursuit of [us]" (*The Hungering Dark*, HarperOne, 1985, pp. 13–14).

Amazing love!

Background Files

The Traitor. Of all the Gospel writers, John is hardest on Judas. That may be because he writes at a time of persecution, when the traitor is worse than the denier. John 9:22 and 12:42-43 both hint that the Christian community has been expelled from the synagogue for their belief in Jesus. In that context, the informant is especially dangerous.

Supper in God's Kingdom. Thus far, when we have talked about God's kingdom—through the Lord's Prayer and the parables and the ministry of Jesus—we have meant the way that God's will gets lived out on earth. Here Jesus tells his disciples, "Truly I tell you, I will never again drink of the fruit of the vine until that day when I drink it new in the kingdom of God" (Mark 14:25). This is a reminder of the other- or after-worldly element in Jesus' teaching about the kingdom.

PICTURING THE STORY

As you watch the story play out in the video, consider:

- What image or moment stands out for you? Why?
- Imagine that you are a spectator at one of these scenes. How do Jesus' actions surprise you? What would you want to ask Jesus?
- What do you think Judas is thinking when he agrees to betray Jesus?
- Where do you see God at work in these stories?
- What questions arise for you?

SINGING THE STORY

Just as the Psalms were the songbook of the people of Israel, so Christians have written and sung hymns and songs to convey the story of Jesus and its meaning.

"Let Us Break Bread Together" (African-American Spiritual)

Let us break bread together on our knees;
Let us break bread together on our knees.

Refrain

When I fall on my knees, with my face to the rising sun,
O Lord, have mercy on me.

Let us drink wine together on our knees;
Let us drink wine together on our knees.
Refrain

Let us praise God together on our knees;
Let us praise God together on our knees.
Refrain

How is Jesus present in our eating and drinking? Do the words of this song speak of past, present, or future to you?

MARK IT

Choose one or more of the following passages to read during the coming week. Mark your readings using the marking method shown below.

Mark 14:35-36	John 15:12-17
Hebrews 5:5-10	Acts 8:26-39

Marking Your Bible

Make notes about the questions and insights you have as you read your Bible. The following symbols might be helpful.

* ∗   A chapter or verse important to me
* !   A new idea
* ✓   A passage to memorize
* ?   Something not clear to me
* ∞   God's love
* ℗   A promise from God
* ≈   Something that connects with my experience
* †   My relationship with God
* ↔   My relationships with others

Next Time

Use the following suggestions to prepare for Session 15.

Read the following passages and review the study notes in *Lutheran Study Bible* for:

* Matthew 26:47—27:66
* Mark 14:43—15:47
* Luke 22:47—23:56
* John 18:1—19:42

Gospels Reading Plan

If you wish to read one entire Gospel or all four Gospels during the sixteen weeks of this study, follow this weekly reading plan.

Week 14: Matthew 24:1—25:46; Mark 14:1-72; Luke 22:1-71; John 19:1-42

CRUCIFY HIM!
Trial and Death

15

When the centurion . . . saw that in this way he breathed his last, he said, "Truly this man was God's Son!"

Jesus' death has drawn, perhaps, more comment than any other event in history. Twenty centuries of Christians have looked to this emblem of Roman torture and execution as the center of their faith. It has been the unlikely inspiration of poets and prophets, monks and ministers.

When Jesus began his journey in the Jordan River, when others joined him along a Galilean Sea, as he healed many and inspired more, no one could have seen this coming. The heaped-to-overflowing life that those who followed him saw now comes to a tragic turn. For his whole life, Jesus has reached out to help. Now, others extend his arms.

Jesus is arrested in the Garden of Gethsemane

- Have you ever been betrayed by a friend? Have you ever betrayed a friend? Describe the feeling of each situation.

AMBUSH IN THE GARDEN (Mark 14:43-50)

The disciples have seen Judas kiss Jesus many times. So, at first, this kiss in the garden looks like friendship. But the crowd following Judas does not look friendly. Angry priests glare and scribes fold their arms. Temple guards lean forward, flashing steel, poised to do their job. To the disciples' horror, this kiss is code. It's the kiss of death.

When guards grab Jesus, a disciple grabs his knife. When he—some say it is Peter—slices off the ear of the chief priest's slave, Jesus protests. One Gospel has him rebuke the violence: "All who take the sword will perish by the sword" (Matthew 26:52). In another, he rebukes resistance to God's plan: "Am I not to drink the cup that the Father has given me?" (John 18:11). Here in Mark, Jesus chides the Jewish leaders: You've seen me teach every day at the temple. Now you corner me like a bandit (14:49).

- When Jesus faced the trial of his life, the trial for his life, his disciples were nowhere to be found. What would have happened had they not abandoned him?

Jesus goes on trial before the council of Jewish leaders

- Why do you think Jesus refuses to defend himself in this trial?

- Through the centuries, Christians have sometimes used passages like this to support their anti-Semitic statements and actions. Are there any non-Jews in this scene? Consider the tragic irony of killing innocent people on the basis of this passage.

Jesus walked into the garden free with eleven friends. He will walk out bound and accompanied by no friends. Mark is candid: "All of them deserted him and fled." Jesus will face his trial—and this will be a trial in every sense of the word—all alone.

A PASSOVER PROSECUTION (Mark 14:53-65)

Next comes the interrogation. The guard hauls Jesus roughly to the high priest's house where, conveniently, the whole council of priests, elders, and scribes has assembled. Prosecutors begin with Jesus' crimes against the temple, calling witnesses to testify that Jesus vowed to tear it down. Their testimony is inconsistent, but that does not slow the momentum toward judgment. Throughout this line of questioning, to his accusers' astonishment and frustration, Jesus remains silent.

Then the prosecutors turn to Jesus' identity. "Are you the Messiah, the Son of the Blessed One?" (14:61). Finally, Jesus helps their cause, saying "I am." That much alone would no doubt have sealed his fate. Messianic pretenders did not fare well with the Jewish hierarchy. The Jews' status with their Roman rulers was always tenuous. The livelihood of the priests depended upon continued harmony. It was in their interest to squelch rabble-rousers.

"I am" would be enough. But Jesus does not stop there. He uses Scripture to broaden his reply. He is Messiah and eternal Son of Man: "You will see the Son of Man seated at the right hand of the Power," and "coming with the clouds of heaven" (Mark 14:62). His accusers are predictably outraged. "Blasphemy!" cries the high priest. The others agree and proceed to take out their holy frustration on Jesus violently, taunting him. At daybreak the rest of the Jewish council rubber-stamps the decision. Jesus will go to Pilate.

It's strange to recall that all this happens to cap off the first day of the festival of Unleavened Bread—an important religious event in Israel. The irony is thick, as it was when Pharisees and Herodians were so angry with Jesus for healing on the Sabbath that they began to plot his death—*on* the Sabbath (Mark 3:6). The religious leaders' hypocrisy threads its way, subtly and unsubtly, through the Gospels. Here it reaches a peak!

A DISCIPLE'S DENIAL

(Mark 14:54, 66-72)

While Jesus faces his accusers courageously inside, Peter sidles up to warm himself by the fire outside. It's not clear why. Curiosity? Maybe. Guilt? Could be. Has he summoned courage to try standing beside Jesus again?

Whatever has brought Peter to the high priest's house, he remains incognito until a servant girl recognizes him: "You also were with Jesus, the man from Nazareth" (Mark 14:67). His resolve dissolves. "I do not know or understand what you are talking about," he says, slinking away to another courtyard. But the servant girl will not relent: "This man is one of them." Again, Peter says no. The third accusation comes from the crowd. They ask, Why else would a Galilean be standing here? This time Peter's denial is vehement: "I do not know this man you are talking about." The rooster's third volley reminds Peter that Jesus had seen this coming. He collapses in tears.

Most of us can't imagine dangerous faith. We live where Christianity is state- and culture-blessed. The most we ever draw, even for the most overt acts of faith, are strange looks. Peter's denials may seem weak to us—at least until we look inside and examine our own frailty. That honest inward glance is our salvation in the face of Peter's failure. It is our only hope to manage a measure of proper humility.

The last word has not yet been spoken—on Peter or on us. Early Christian tradition has it that thirty-five years later Peter faced another trial in Rome before a greater power than a high priest and a servant girl. When Nero's henchmen asked, Peter got his second chance, and this time the Holy Spirit helped him. You bet I was with him! he said. And he was crucified for it. But when it came time to hoist him on a cross, he said, "I don't deserve his glory. Put me upside down." Humility indeed.

Peter denies Jesus

- Can you relate to Peter? What situations in your life tempt you to deny your faith?

- You may know that later Jesus does not reject Peter because of his denials; rather he calls on him to take the lead amongst his apostles (see John 21:15-19). What does this say to you about Jesus? About your life of faith?

THE VOICE OF THE PEOPLE (Mark 15:1-15)

Pilate cares nothing about the religious nuances of the Jews. He is Roman. Jewish religion is at best an inconvenience to him. When irate Jewish leaders arrive with their prisoner, he couldn't care less about Jesus' blasphemy. His concern is Jesus' potential to disrupt the famous Roman order and peace. That's why the Jewish leaders translate to Pilate in language that might interest him: This Jesus claims to be king of the Jews.

Pilate turns their charge into a question for Jesus: "Are you the King of the Jews?" Jesus replies, "You say so." To the priests' other accusations, Jesus offers no reply. His silence amazes Pilate, who sees through the priests' motives (Mark 15:10) and remains unconvinced of Jesus' guilt.

Custom offers Pilate an out. He can legally release one Jewish prisoner during the Passover feast. "Do you want me to release for you the King of the Jews?" But the priests have lathered up the crowd in advance. They instead ask for a dangerous insurrectionist. Give us Barabbas! The mob drowns out Pilate's plea on Jesus' behalf. "Crucify him!"

Ultimately Pilate relents and pleases the crowd. Soldiers flog Jesus and then, since they know the charge, mock him with royal dress—a purple cloak, a crown of thorns—as they beat him more: "Hail, King of the Jews!" When they've had their sport, they strip him, commandeer a bystander to carry his cross, and set out for Golgotha.

Pilate gives in to the people's call to crucify Jesus

- Pilate could have refused to sentence Jesus to death by crucifixion. Why didn't he?

- Can you hear yourself shouting the words "Crucify him"? Would you have been silent? Would you have opposed?

DARK AT MIDDAY (Mark 15:16-47)

Good Friday has reached its central moment. Jesus' journey from Gethsemane to the high priest to Pilate to the soldiers and now to the cross has been a constant rush of activity. Now everything stops. For three long, dark hours he hangs on the cross—hangs there beneath a label that tells his crime: "The King of the Jews."

Each Gospel emphasizes an aspect of this strange, excruciating, complex moment of crucifixion. Luke and John paint Jesus in continued command of himself and those around him. He receives the criminal's plea, "Jesus, remember me, . . ." and replies with grace, "Today you will be with me in Paradise" (Luke 23:43). He watches out for his mother, supplying a stand-in for himself: "Woman, here is your son." And to John: "Here is your mother"

Jesus is crucified under the sign "King of the Jews"

(John 19:26-27). Jesus' composure continues through his dying: "It is finished." (John 19:30) and "Father, into your hands I commend my spirit" (Luke 23:46). John and Luke each capture one element of the cross.

Mark and Matthew tell the story of the cross more briefly, and they emphasize Jesus' anguish. They hear him shout words of dereliction from Psalm 22, "My God, my God, why have you forsaken me?" (Matthew 27:46; Mark 15:34). Their bystanders mistake Jesus' Aramaic words as a cry for Elijah and then belittle him for it. The next sound we hear is an inarticulate cry, this time as Jesus dies. Their scene shifts briefly to the temple, where Jesus' death splits open the enormous curtain that separates worshipers from God's direct presence (the Holy of Holies). Matthew and Mark isolate Jesus' agony.

- The Gospels have been telling us who Jesus is. What does the crucifixion say about who Jesus is?

The scene culminates, ironically, with the words of a Roman soldier. It's been his job to stand guard at the execution. Presumably it is not his first, but this death stands out to him. The centurion has not been privy to the arguing over Jesus' crime. He's heard neither priests nor Pilate. He cannot, of course, see the temple curtain tear. The centurion's only acquaintance with Jesus is with what Bernard of Clairvaux will one day call his "dying sorrow." But somehow the death is enough. Seeing Jesus breathe his last, this nameless Roman soldier gazes up and speaks words that echo the first sentence of Mark's Gospel: "Truly this man was God's Son!" (Mark 15:39)

- As you stand at the foot of the cross looking up, what do you see?

PICTURING THE STORY

As you watch the drama leading to Jesus' crucifixion play out, consider:

- What image or moment stands out for you? Why?
- Was anything new or surprising to you?
- Imagine yourself in one of the scenes described in this session. Where are you? What are you seeing?
- Where do you see God at work in these events?
- What would you like to ask Jesus or any other person in these scenes?

SINGING THE STORY

Just as the Psalms were the songbook of the people of Israel, so Christians have written and sung hymns and songs to convey the story of Jesus and its meaning.

"O Sacred Head, Now Wounded" (Paul Gerhardt, 1607–1676, based on Arnulf of Louvain, d. 1250; tr. composite)

O sacred head, now wounded,
with grief and shame weighed down,
now scornfully surrounded
with thorns, thine only crown;
O sacred head, what glory,
what bliss till now was thine!
Yet, though despised and gory,
I joy to call thee mine.

What language shall I borrow
to thank thee, dearest friend,
for this thy dying sorrow,
thy pity without end?
Oh, make me thine forever,
and should I fainting be,
Lord, let me never, never
outlive my love to thee.

Why does the ancient writer see beauty in a head bloodied by a crown of thorns? What words do you have for the one who died to save?

MARK IT

Choose one or more of the following passages to read during the coming week. Mark your readings using the marking method shown below.

Mark 15:37-39
1 Corinthians 1:18

Isaiah 52:13—53:12
2 Corinthians 5:16-21

Marking Your Bible

Make notes about the questions and insights you have as you read your Bible. The following symbols might be helpful.

* ✻ A chapter or verse important to me
* ! A new idea
* ✓ A passage to memorize
* ? Something not clear to me
* ∞ God's love
* Ⓟ A promise from God
* ≈ Something that connects with my experience
* † My relationship with God
* ↔ My relationships with others

Next Time

Use the following suggestions to prepare for Session 16.

Read the following passages and review the study notes in *Lutheran Study Bible* for:
- Matthew 28:1-20
- Mark 16:1-8 [9-20]
- Luke 24:1-53
- John 20:1—21:25

Gospels Reading Plan

If you wish to read one entire Gospel or all four Gospels during the sixteen weeks of this study, follow this weekly reading plan.

Week 15: Matthew 26:1—27:66; Mark 15:1-47; Luke 23:1-56; John 20:1-31

A SUNDAY SURPRISE

Resurrection

16

Why do you look for the living among the dead? He is not here, but has risen.

"Christ Is Risen!" "He Is Risen, Indeed!" This centuries-old Easter greeting between Christians expresses the surprise and joy of resurrection. Dead people aren't supposed to become un-dead. An old adage pairs death with taxes as the two human certainties. But all four Gospels (and the rest of the New Testament) boldly proclaim that Jesus of Nazareth has risen from the dead. After Jesus' disciples have endured the long and mournful Friday and Saturday nights, imagine that Sunday morning!

The mysterious, powerful event of resurrection marked the early Christians in two important ways. First, through it they came to believe that Jesus had conquered death, so that they need not be afraid to die. Second, they believed that Jesus had much more work to do in the world, all of which he would accomplish through them. When he appears to the disciples after his resurrection, Jesus says, "Peace be with you" and then, "Go therefore and make disciples."

Jesus speaks that assurance and that commission as freshly and directly to us as he spoke it to those first disciples. Let's find our way into that ancient scene with them.

EMPTY TOMB (Luke 24:1-12)

Jesus' resurrection was a complete surprise to his friends. Luke tells us that Joanna, Mary Magdalene, James's mother, Mary, and a few other women see the empty tomb first, not because they have been expectantly waiting for dawn, but because they have prepared spices for the corpse. In fact, not one of Jesus' followers in any of the Gospel accounts waited up that first Easter Eve or rose expectantly on that first Easter morn. Not one expected this

*Jesus has risen, but
for the disciples
the resurrection is
unrecognized*

- Would you have been up early
  to check for resurrection?
  Would you have been with
  the women tending the
  body or with the disciples in
  mourning?

- Have you ever experienced
  resurrection in your life?
  When? How?

resurrection, even after each of the Gospels portrays Jesus telling them ahead of time that he would be crucified and rise.

Surely the gruesome events of Calvary were traumatic. The hope of Jesus' followers had been dashed. And their own performance under pressure had left much to be desired. Peter denied Jesus. All the others fled the Garden of Gethsemane when Jesus was arrested.

Whether from grief or forgetting, when these women see an empty tomb and two angelic men, they are flummoxed and terrified. The men in dazzling array remind them, "Remember how he told you . . . ?" (Luke 24:6). Their jogged memories do at last work, and now they are excited by the prospect. The women hurry back to the disciples and tell what they've seen and heard, but now the disciples don't believe it. "These words seemed to them an idle tale." Those are the words of grieved men. Only Peter wants to investigate, and the empty tomb leaves him amazed.

*The resurrected Jesus
appears*

THE ROAD TO EMMAUS (Luke 24:13-49)

Who would be first to see Jesus? Details of the resurrection vary across the five New Testament accounts. If, as many authorities believe, the Gospel as written by Mark ends at 16:8, that's before Jesus appears to anyone, and it has the women running scared from the empty tomb. In Matthew, the women meet Jesus on their way back to tell the disciples of an empty tomb. In John, Mary Magdalene sees Jesus first, near the tomb, but doesn't recognize him until he speaks her name. And the Apostle Paul reports that Jesus appears first to Cephas (Peter), then to the twelve, then "to more than five hundred brothers and sisters at one time" (1 Corinthians 15:3-8).

Luke tells of two dejected followers of Jesus on a Sunday walk from Jerusalem to Emmaus. When Jesus joins them on the road, they, like Mary Magdalene in John's Gospel, don't immediately recognize him. Grief-stricken as they are, his questions seem almost to offend them: "Are you the only stranger in Jerusalem who does not know the things that have taken place there in these days?" (24:18). But when Jesus persists, they pour out their grief to him: "We had hoped that he was the one to redeem Israel." They tell of an empty tomb, but no one has yet seen Jesus.

There follows a lecture that we Bible people would love to have on DVD: Jesus chronicles for these two all that the Scripture has said about him, from Moses all the way through the prophets. But still they don't awaken to who he is. Jesus begins to walk away, but it is late in the day, so they hospitably invite him to stay with them. The light of recognition does not dawn until dinner, when Jesus blesses bread and breaks it. Suddenly, two things happen: they recognize Jesus, and he disappears from view. Mysterious! He leaves them with a gift: "Were not our hearts burning within us?"

Our two guys hurry back to the disciples in Jerusalem. But they've barely started their story when Jesus appears again, like history's greatest visual aid. After initially thinking he's a ghost, the eleven ultimately recognize him, and he repeats his biblical lesson for them.

Centuries of Christians have discovered that their eyes also open when Jesus breaks bread. That's another thing we do Sunday after Sunday, because we know that our ancient brothers on that Emmaus road were not the last to feel their hearts burn.

- Why don't the men on the road recognize Jesus?

- When have your "eyes of faith" been opened? What did you see?

- An *epiphany* is a sudden moment of realization or clarity. What has prompted epiphanies of faith in your life?

GO! (Matthew 28:16-20; Acts 1:8)

What's next? We might imagine that's the pressing concern for the disciples after the women tell them, "We've seen the Lord!" (Matthew 28:8). What's next? There are options. The disciples could simply return to their old separate lives—to fishing and tax collecting and the like—enlightened by the truth that God has loved them through their departed friend Jesus. Or they could stay together and become a sort of monastic community, celebrating their heart-warmings and remembering the good old days with Jesus. They could continue Jesus' work in Galilee and set up a church there. There are options. We don't get access to their thought bubble, but surely in the face of resurrection they are thinking.

What's next? When Jesus appears to them in Galilee it becomes clear that he has asked and answered the same question. "Go therefore and make disciples of all nations." Jesus has a job for them, and it is no small order. All of the amazing things of which Matthew's Gospel tells happened within the

Jesus sends his followers into the world

county-sized land of Galilee and the city of Jerusalem. Now he is directing them to "all nations."

Are they up to it? At first glance, we'd have to guess not. After all, with the resurrected Jesus standing in front of them, "They worshiped him; but some doubted" (Matthew 28:17). They doubted? If you were in charge and you knew the size of the task ahead, you'd probably do some personnel work and lay off a few disciples. But Jesus doesn't bat an eye. He tells all of them, "Go."

• How can Jesus use disciples who doubt (Matthew 28:17) to reach the whole world (Matthew 28:18-20)?

• What does Jesus mean when he says, "I am with you always"?

What gives him confidence in them? Precisely that it will not be just them. "Remember, I am with you always, to the end of the age" (28:20). The resurrected one will go with them. Luke's report in Acts 1:8 has Jesus do a similar thing: "You will receive power when the Holy Spirit has come upon you; and you will be my witnesses in Jerusalem, in all Judea and Samaria, and to the ends of the earth." The task is huge, but the presence and power of Jesus will be with them as they go.

It's easy for us and for our churches to forget the second part of Jesus' call. It's easy for us to forget that the presence and power of Christ, God with us, is ours too. We go forth, sometimes fully aware and sometimes not noticing that the holy wind that blew out of that ancient tomb is at our backs too.

Background Files

Ghosts and Fish. As part of Jesus' demonstration that they are experiencing him and not a ghost, he asks the Emmaus followers for solid food.

In the Temple. The Gospel of Luke ends where Acts will begin: "They worshiped [Jesus], and returned to Jerusalem with great joy; and they were continually in the temple blessing God." The disciples assumed that their devotion to Jesus could and would continue as a part of the Jewish community in Jerusalem. It won't be until the eighth chapter of Acts, after Stephen is stoned, that that habit changes.

The Great Commission. The same Greek phrase, *ta ethna,* which appears in both Matthew 28:19 and Luke 24:47 means either "the nations" or "the Gentiles." Although Jesus told his followers to make disciples of all nations, Acts indicates that they did not immediately seek to evangelize Gentiles (non-Jews). This begins to change in Acts 10 when Peter baptizes a Gentile centurion; later the Apostle Paul takes the gospel to Gentiles throughout the Roman world.

Geography. Locate Emmaus, Jerusalem, and Galilee on the map "Palestine in Jesus' Time," page 2109 in *Lutheran Study Bible.*

PICTURING THE STORY

As you watch resurrection appearances depicted, consider:

- Do you see anything in a new way? If so, what?
- What questions are raised for you?
- Imagine being present in one of the scenes described in this session. What do you think of Jesus' words? Are you frightened? Excited? Uncertain?
- Where do you see God at work in these events?
- What image of Jesus stands out for you in all of his "story"? Why?

SINGING THE STORY

Just as the Psalms were the songbook of the people of Israel, so Christians have written and sung hymns and songs to convey the story of Jesus and its meaning.

"Jesus Christ Is Risen Today" (Latin carol, 14th century, tr. J. Walsh, *Lyra Davidica,* 1708, alt.)

Jesus Christ is ris'n today, Alleluia!
our triumphant holy day, Alleluia!
who did once upon the cross, Alleluia!
suffer to redeem our loss. Alleluia!

How do you express the joy of Easter? How are cross and empty tomb forever linked?

MARK IT

Choose one or more of the following passages to read during the coming week. Mark your readings using the marking method shown below.

Matthew 28:18-20	1 Corinthians 15:54-57
Romans 8:31-39	1 Peter 1:3-9

Marking Your Bible

Make notes about the questions and insights you have as you read your Bible. The following symbols might be helpful.

* A chapter or verse important to me
! A new idea
√ A passage to memorize
? Something not clear to me
∞ God's love
℗ A promise from God
≈ Something that connects with my experience
† My relationship with God
↔ My relationships with others

Gospels Reading Plan

If you wish to read one entire Gospel or all four Gospels during the sixteen weeks of this study, follow this weekly reading plan.

Week 16: Matthew 28:1-20; Mark 16:1-8 [9-20]; Luke 24:1-53; John 21:1-25